aim high, achieve more

ASCD MEMBER BOOK

Many ASCD members received this book as a
member benefit upon its initial release.

Learn more at: **www.ascd.org/memberbooks**

aim high, achieve more

How to Transform Urban Schools Through Fearless Leadership

Yvette Jackson & Veronica McDermott

Alexandria, Virginia USA

1703 N. Beauregard St. • Alexandria, VA 22311-1714 USA
Phone: 800-933-2723 or 703-578-9600 • Fax: 703-575-5400
Website: www.ascd.org • E-mail: member@ascd.org
Author guidelines: www.ascd.org/write

Gene R. Carter, *Executive Director;* Ed Milliken, *Interim Chief Program Development Officer;*
Carole Hayward, *Interim Publisher;* Genny Ostertag, *Acquisitions Editor;* Julie Houtz, *Director,*
Book Editing & Production; Miriam Goldstein, *Editor;* Sima Nasr, *Senior Graphic Designer;*
Mike Kalyan, *Production Manager;* Cynthia Stock, *Typesetter*

Copyright © 2012 ASCD. All rights reserved. It is illegal to reproduce copies of this work in print or
electronic format (including reproductions displayed on a secure intranet or stored in a retrieval system
or other electronic storage device from which copies can be made or displayed) without the prior
written permission of the publisher. By purchasing only authorized electronic or print editions and
not participating in or encouraging piracy of copyrighted materials, you support the rights of authors
and publishers. Readers who wish to duplicate material copyrighted by ASCD may do so for a small
fee by contacting the Copyright Clearance Center (CCC), 222 Rosewood Dr., Danvers, MA 01923,
USA (phone: 978-750-8400; fax: 978-646-8600; web: www.copyright.com). For requests to reprint or
to inquire about site licensing options, contact ASCD Permissions at www.ascd.org/permissions, or
permission@ascd.org, or 703-575-5749. For a list of vendors authorized to license ASCD e-books to
institutions, see www.ascd.org/epubs. Send translation inquiries to translations@ascd.org.

Printed in the United States of America. Cover art © 2012 by ASCD. ASCD publications present a
variety of viewpoints. The views expressed or implied in this book should not be interpreted as official
positions of the Association.

All web links in this book are correct as of the publication date below but may have become inactive or
otherwise modified since that time. If you notice a deactivated or changed link, please e-mail books@
ascd.org with the words "Link Update" in the subject line. In your message, please specify the web link,
the book title, and the page number on which the link appears.

ASCD Member Book, No. FY12-9 (Aug. 2012, P). ASCD Member Books mail to Premium (P), Select
(S), and Institutional Plus (I+) members on this schedule: Jan., PSI+; Feb., P; Apr., PSI+; May, P; July,
PSI+; Aug., P; Sept., PSI+; Nov., PSI+; Dec., P. Select membership was formerly known as Comprehen-
sive membership.

PAPERBACK ISBN: 978-1-4166-1467-8   ASCD product #112015

Also available as an e-book (see Books in Print for the ISBNs).

Quantity discounts: 10–49 copies, 10%; 50+ copies, 15%; for 1,000 or more copies, call 800-933-2723,
ext. 5634, or 703-575-5634. For desk copies: www.ascd.org/deskcopy.

Library of Congress Cataloging-in-Publication Data

Jackson, Yvette.
  Aim high, achieve more : how to transform urban schools through fearless leadership /
Yvette Jackson and Veronica McDermott.
     p. cm.
  Includes bibliographical references and index.
  ISBN 978-1-4166-1467-8 (pbk. : alk. paper)
  1. School management and organization—United States. 2. Urban schools—United States—
Administration. 3. School improvement programs—United States. 4. Educational leadership—
United States. I. McDermott, Veronica. II. Title.
  LB2805.J17 2012
  371.2'011—dc23
                                                                    2012017884

This book is about—and for—children.

It is about—and for—Carlos in San Francisco,
Amos in Newark, and Tanesha in Atlanta.

It is about—and for—the scores of children who live and learn
in the deepest recesses of our nation's inner cities and the
often-forgotten pockets of rural and suburban poverty.

It is about—and for—students who arrive at school carrying bulging
backpacks of debilitating obstacles and shattered promises but who
want nothing more than to have their hopes sustained and nurtured.

It is about—and for—educators who refuse to accept the status quo and
are searching for ways to transform their schools into oases of success.

Over the years, we have met and worked alongside many educators who
struggle to transform the learning lives of students like Carlos, Amos, and
Tanesha. These educators and their students have taught us what it means
to aim for self-actualization and self-directed learning every hour of every
day, even when the odds are stacked against them. The optimism, fortitude,
and fearlessness of these educators and students have inspired us.

We dedicate this book to all who have worked on behalf of children, to
all who decide to join this movement, and to all the children who will
reap the benefits of living their learning lives fearlessly and joyfully.

aim high, achieve more

Acknowledgments

This book is about journeys: the ones we have been on and the ones we are encouraging others to take. As we reflect on the journey that led us to write this book, we recognize the many people along the way who affirmed our efforts, inspired us, and mediated our thinking and behavior. Among these people are the students, teachers, and administrators with whom we have worked. We thank them for providing such clear examples of fearlessness. We also thank all of the regional directors, mentors, and researchers associated with NUA who share with us the vision of founder and president Eric Cooper.

We would not have been able to "aim high" had it not been for the affirmation, inspiration, and mediation of family members who cheered for us on the sidelines when they were not lovingly providing direct support.

. . . .

I would like to especially recognize the family members who so often played the role of soul friends, muses, and ministers: my son and daughter-in-law, Liam and Nina, whose affirmations often came with a good dose of humor; my husband, Jim, whose inspiration is driven by his extraordinary capacity to synthesize disparate elements into seamless sense; my daughter and son-in-law, Mairi and

Marlon, whose mediation helped me find my voice and took me on incredible journeys into new theoretical and philosophical landscapes, pointing out vistas of ideas I never dreamed I would visit, much less understand or be able to "name" accurately; and my mother and father, who in their own way have been the architects who set the whole process in motion.

Veronica McDermott

I would like to thank my husband and family for the eternal support they give me in undertaking the mission I have dedicated my life to: being the voice for the children in urban school districts.

I continue to thank Reuven Feuerstein for the honor of being his student and for the inspiration and affirmation he has given me over the years and across the many miles to undertake this mission.

Yvette Jackson

Introduction

> A different world cannot be created by indifferent people.
>
> *—Horace Mann*

Fearless Leaders

The fearless leaders we know—and we know many—are just like you. They are district office administrators, building principals, coaches, and teacher leaders of various types, some of whom are anointed with titles, many of whom are not. They work in schools under-resourced and overburdened, often located in the deepest recesses of our nation's inner cities, but also found on country roads and suburban lanes. They serve disproportionately large numbers of children who live in poverty, children who come from immigrant families, and children who face racism daily. They are also ordinary educators committed to proving that demographics need not be destiny (Cooper, 2005). If they have given up on anything, it is the false hope that outside resources will ever be directed their way in sufficient amounts to make a difference. Instead, they have mined the resources that exist within their schools—the dedication of their teachers, the dreams of their students' families, the deep untapped potential of their students, and their own driving desire to make a difference—and they have created oases of success despite the weight of demographic obstacles and the wreckage outside their doors (Jackson, 2011).

Choose Fearlessness

Educators have two choices: to be fearful or to be fearless. This book is written for those who choose to be fearless, who want to rekindle the passion that brought them to education in the first place, who recognize the power of working with others to create a different world with their students, and who have the stamina to take on a task beset with obstacles, a task likely to draw fire from vested interests, and a task cynics will say is impossible. In other words, this book is a call to action for those committed to creating an oasis of success in what is often the bleak landscape of urban education.

Despite how popular media and many policymakers choose to portray urban education, those of us dedicated to working in urban schools know that there are legions of committed, compassionate, and courageous people who have chosen to provide hope, optimism, and opportunity for students who are made to feel school-dependent.

We deliberately use the phrase "made to feel school-dependent" to amplify the fact that students come to school with an abundance of different forms of knowledge and understanding that become discredited by the types of knowledge that are considered valid by school. In a sense, these students depend on us to help them shatter the notion that they are somehow deficient, when they, like all students, arrive at the schoolhouse door brimming with rich ways of knowing, doing, and being.

As we all know, words matter: language frames the way we see the world and the way the world sees us. We know the transformative, exhilarating, affirming power of the right word said at the right time, as well as the spirit-crushing damage of the wrong word persistently used to set limits on who we are and who we can become. By choosing to call our students school-dependent, we trumpet our recognition of the realities and conditions our students face daily, both inside and outside school (Cooper, 2005).

But there is more. This term reminds us that our role is to bridge the divide that separates students from their birthright: a high-quality education that enables them to realize their vast potential. It renews our original sense of purpose and emboldens us to provide the conditions that will enable all students, not just the lucky few, to reach high levels of intellectual performance and to become self-actualized and self-directed learners (Jackson, 2011). These conditions tap into and develop who students are, instead of forcing them to fit into a system that denies their heritage and ways of being.

You Now Have a Guidebook

Being a fearless leader requires more than just a rekindled sense of passion, faith in your ability to make change, and a heightened sense of urgency to get on with the work; it also requires real skills. Use this book as your guide as you go about turning an underperforming school into an oasis of success. The journey is not meant to be undertaken solo, so we wrote this guidebook to support group investigations. Use it as an open invitation to your staff to join you on this journey of transformation.

Components of the Book

This book, based on our experiences with urban educators throughout the United States, is organized the way most guidebooks are: it begins with preparations for the journey, suggests an itinerary designed to ensure you do not miss anything important during the trip, and ends with what you are likely to experience at your final destination. It offers practical suggestions and examples gleaned from real-world experiences and the reflections of deep thinkers in various fields of inquiry, snapshots and anecdotes of others who have taken similar journeys, points of interest along the way, and ideas and activities that will support you and your team as you beat a path to a fully realized and vibrant learning environment.

We recognize the special complexities inherent in the transformation of urban schools. In preparing this book, we have kept these complexities in mind.

We are convinced that a successful journey requires leadership courageous enough to

• Adopt a high-definition, panoramic view of the current situation. Taking this view requires you to tap into the multiple perspectives and strengths of a leadership team made up of important stakeholders, including students.

• Redefine your school "reality" in terms that proudly recognize the unlimited and underused potential that exists in your school and community.

• Boldly mediate for, nurture, demonstrate, and defend the high intellectual performances of urban students and the teachers on whom they depend.

• Unflinchingly jettison obsolete, isolating, and soul-crushing institutional arrangements that prevent schools from becoming enriching, supportive, and creative communities (Jackson, 2011).

To help you prepare for the journey and understand the lay of the land, the first three chapters answer three crucial questions: What is fearless leading? To what are fearless leaders committed? Why are fearless leaders needed?

The second section of the book addresses the routes fearless leaders take to reach their destination. A major premise of this book is that fearless leaders can purposely reorient themselves as architects of their schools' destiny. The architect is one of four leadership stances that dramatically alter how leaders see themselves, how others see them, and how they approach the work of transformation. Once fearless leaders understand that they are the architects of their schools' destiny, they are capable of transforming that destiny by reorienting themselves through the other stances assumed by fearless leaders: soul friends, muses, and ministers (Jackson & McDermott, 2009). They create the supports that encourage teachers to believe in their students' potential and in their own ability to nurture that potential (Jackson, 2011). Chapters 4 through 7 describe how each of these stances propels fearless leaders to take dramatically different routes to transformation. These routes are *affirmation, inspiration,* and *mediation.*

Chapter 4 explains how, in their roles as soul friends, fearless leaders affirm others in deep, insightful ways. Chapter 5 addresses how, in their roles as muses, fearless leaders inspire others to arrive at a shared commitment to change. Chapter 6 explains how fearless leaders mediate, or minister, to the needs of students and teachers. Through targeted mediation, learning and teaching is transformed into what we call the *Pedagogy of Confidence®:* the artful use of the science of learning to create high operational practices that elicit high levels of intellectual performance from all students (Jackson, 2011). Chapter 7 takes an important side trip to highlight one highly transformative act of mediation: amplifying student voice.

But these routes tell only half the story. If fearless leading constitutes the steps along the way to a destination, the destination is learning and teaching situated in a fearless environment we call a *Mediative Learning Community®,* a shared culture of positive relationships and cordial reciprocity between educators and learners (Jackson, 2011). Chapter 8 presents an overview of the elements of a Mediative Learning Community—a mini-portrait of what fearless leaders are likely to have created as a result of this journey—and Chapter 9 provides an extended example of a school on its way to becoming a Mediative Learning Community.

By its very nature, transformation requires that each school create its own roadmap for change. To help in this process, each chapter ends with activities that will help your leadership team prepare for the journey of transformation. The reflections and activities that end each chapter are intended to be group explorations for your leadership team.

As your team conducts these explorations, several important changes will begin to take place. Your team will develop the means to enact transformation in your school. You will experience the euphoria that springs from transformed beliefs and common understanding. You will see yourselves as strong, capable, and necessary agents of transformation. You will develop a sense of fearlessness and the skills necessary to be fearless. You will prepare yourselves to embark on the transformation journey.

Overview of the Journey

The Departure Point

Today's urban schools are often defined as failures, and too many urban educators live in fear of the repercussions of that negative label: increasingly punitive sanctions, loss of respect, even loss of livelihood. Not surprisingly, this fear is palpable, especially to the students whose school experiences are led by educators shackled by fear. The effects of this fear on students and teachers alike are far-reaching: fear affects people's physical, mental, and emotional well-being and functioning (Jackson, 2011).

Fearless leaders work daily to counteract the negative stereotypes that others use to define and limit them. These stereotypes often become the internal maps that people use to perceive how things "ought" to work (Roxburgh, 2010). One of the first tasks of fearless leaders, then, is to tear up these outdated, dead-end maps and begin making a new map that charts new territory and takes students and teachers to life-affirming and life-sustaining places.

The Itinerary

Every school will begin this journey from a different place and face different obstacles as it navigates the bumpy terrain of transformation. Although we lay out three specific routes to smooth the way—affirmation, inspiration, and mediation—we recognize that with any complicated journey, routes intertwine and intersect, and travelers may deliberately switch routes to meet a need or deal with an unexpected impediment. We hope you will explore the proposed itineraries, see how each is essential, and, in the end, recognize the complex relationship among them and the transformative power inherent in following each route.

Reorientation in a New Landscape

Often, commencing a new journey requires specialized equipment. You cannot go whitewater rafting without a raft, a wetsuit, and a paddle. Similarly, you cannot fearlessly transform a school without specialized emotional, attitudinal, and dispositional "equipment." Worn-out conceptions of leadership will not equip you to be fearless. Instead, we offer four defining metaphors that reorient leaders and enable them to pursue leadership fearlessly, in their roles as architects, soul friends, muses, and ministers. Changing how leaders define themselves—and how they allow others to define them—is crucial.

We have chosen metaphors outside the normal lexicon of leadership for a reason. Metaphors, although often unnoticed, act as powerful guiding forces in our everyday lives (Lackoff & Johnson, 2003). They are a window into how we see ourselves and how we operate in the world. Educators who view themselves as warriors mowing down opposition on a battlefield present a very different face to the world than do those who view themselves as gardeners cultivating a field of flowers. Both metaphors are powerful, but the images they suggest and the types of actions they foster are diametrically different. The metaphors leaders use reveal the manner in which they approach their work.

The Destination

Geographic oases stand out as isolated pockets of diverse vegetation in an inhospitable environment that cannot be depended on to provide the resources needed to create a thriving, life-sustaining world. To sustain themselves, oases tap into unseen resources that reside under them: underground rivers, aquifers, and other hidden sources of water. Sometimes these sources spring naturally to the surface; often, they require human-made interventions, such as wells, to begin the transformation from a dry patch of earth to a flourishing source of renewal, food, and shelter. Migrating birds scatter seeds collected from the fruits of the oasis to other parts of the desert primed to accept them, thus extending the impact of the oasis outside its confines.

Schools that are oases of success have gone through a similar transformative process. They have abandoned the notion that outside help is on its way and instead have tapped into the hidden potential and rich resources that exist in their buildings: their faculties, their students, their parents, their communities. They are organized around a single goal: high intellectual performances for all students (Jackson, 2011). They recognize that their role is to nurture and support students as they grow into confident and competent learners, and they are not burdened by the need to fit these learners into notions of learning imposed by others. Just as in nature, mediation is required to begin the process of creating an oasis of success. In our experience, that mediation springs from the vision, will, and skills of the school's leaders to "AIM" high: *a*ffirm, *i*nspire, and *m*ediate.

Introducing Your Guides

Why take on the challenge of transforming your school when the odds are stacked against you? We ask ourselves the same question all the time, and although we come to this work from different personal and professional experiences, we have reached the same conclusion: we do this work because we believe in the power of optimism. We have seen optimism work wonders in schools all over the United States. We know that optimism is the life force of change, and we know that leaders are the life force of optimism.

How did we get to a place where we are willing to take a chance on optimism? Both products of the booming parochial school mania that swept New York City during the 1950s, we were, indeed, parochial. Despite our geographical proximity, our paths could never have crossed when we were growing up. We occupied two narrowly defined, circumspect solitudes: Yvette, multiracial (using the classification of African American), the product of a divorced teacher and a businessman; and Veronica, second-generation working-class Italian American. Race and class kept us apart in one of the most diverse cities in the world, a city that was clearly segregated in the 1950s and, unfortunately, is even more segregated today.

Our professional paths were also different. Yvette paved a career in public schools in urban settings, including New York City, where she was Director of Gifted Programs and then Executive Director of Instruction and Professional Development for New York City Public Schools. Veronica spent her time in what was touted to baby boomers as the "idyllic" setting of suburban Long Island. Having experienced the educational whimsy associated with a wealthy school district, she eventually went on to become the superintendent of a school district struggling to provide high-quality educational experiences to a largely working-class community with an ever-increasing number of immigrant students—undocumented, non-English-speaking, and, often, unwanted.

Our Mission: Eradicating the Crime of Squandered Potential

Our experiences highlighted what we came to realize was the crime of squandered potential. Through no fault of their own, certain children are denied access to the rigorous education, the high standards, and the crucial resources that would enable them to cultivate their potential and meet high standards. The perpetrator in the crime of squandered potential is a systemic lack of opportunity, often fueled by lack of belief (Jackson, 2011).

We currently work with the National Urban Alliance for Effective Education (NUA). For more than 20 years, the NUA has partnered with school districts all over the United States that are willing to take a chance on renewing under-performing schools. NUA was a pioneer in urban school renewal years before the enactment of the federally mandated interventions currently sweeping the nation. Our efforts focus on professional learning designed to renew teachers' belief in the potential of their students to achieve high levels of intellectual per-formance as well as in their own abilities to deliver the kind of pedagogy that leads to increased student outcomes (Jackson, 2011). Our work also addresses the institutional and structural arrangements that define and delimit students and teachers. Our experiences convinced us that the key ingredient for school renewal—for eradicating the crime of squandered potential—is fearless leader-ship. Fearless leaders fueled by optimism are dedicated to creating an educa-tional oasis for their students, for the teachers on whom those students depend, and for themselves.

Our mission, then, is simple. How do we support principals to become pathfinder principals—principals who amass a team capable of cutting through negative and destructive forces; who place affirmation, inspiration, and media-tion as the centerpiece of their belief and operating systems; and who use their strengths as architects, soul friends, muses, and ministers to cultivate the envi-ronment that enables their schools to flourish? These oases are schools where the artful science of learning leads to high operational practices that fuel high intellectual performances so that students, teachers, and administrators become fearless, self-directed, and, eventually, self-actualized learners (Jackson, 2011).

A tall order? Yes, but one that every child deserves, and one that urban lead-ers need to cultivate with intensity and intentionality.

We began this introduction with a quotation from Horace Mann: "A differ-ent world cannot be created by indifferent people." Fearless leaders are anything but indifferent. They are consumed, emboldened, and animated by the desire to create a different world for their students. The purpose of this book is to provide fearless leaders with the skills and the confidence to lead their schools on a jour-ney to a different world, one they know is right for them, one they create with others, and one that reflects shared dreams, values, and aspirations.

If one advances confidently in the direction of his dreams,
and endeavors to live the life which he has imagined, he will
meet with a success unexpected in common hours.

—*Henry David Thoreau*

Part 1

Preparation

Few people set off on a journey without first asking some essential questions, such as, "What is there to see and do where I am going? What is the best way to get there? Will I need a passport or a visa? What should I pack? Do I need insurance? What is the weather like? What kind of currency do I need? When is the best time to go?"

The three chapters in this first section provide ways of thinking about three similarly key questions to prepare you and your team for this journey:

- What is fearless leading?
- To what are fearless leaders committed?
- Why are fearless leaders needed?

The journey to becoming a fearless leader is not a simple one. These grounding questions will enable your team to come to a common understanding about the essentials before you embark on your journey.

1

···

What Is Fearless Leading?

You may feel afraid. You do not have to act afraid.

—Dan Millman

Key Considerations

- What does a school on its way to becoming an oasis of success look like?
- What does it mean to AIM for high intellectual performances?
- Who are the key players in transforming a school?
- What are the vital signs of fearlessness that, when confidently implemented, block power leaks?

Snapshot: One School's Journey

At 7:00 a.m. on February 11, 2011, more than 30 New York City educators boarded a bus in the Bronx to travel to Bridgeport, Connecticut, where they would visit the Beardsley School. This K–6 school has the dubious distinction of having been on the Schools in Need of Improvement list before the advent of No Child Left Behind (NCLB).

Despite being located in one of the richest counties in one of the richest states in the United States, Beardsley School, like many of its sister schools in the city of Bridgeport, serves a community saddled with the ravages of poverty. Close to 100 percent of students qualify for free or reduced-price lunch. Forty percent of students identify as black, and just below 60 percent of students identify as Hispanic or Latino/Latina, many of them coming from homes in which English is not the primary language. The school building is well over 100 years old and is sandwiched between a car repair shop and a ramshackle clapboard house. Teachers whose classrooms face the house often have to close their shades to shield students from whatever is happening on the front porch.

In 2002, when Amy Marshall came on as principal, Beardsley students' families were doing all they could to find other schools for their children. Yet even with the continual flight, occupancy was at 135 percent, a condition that contributed to short tempers and long suspensions. One prominent community member, echoing a widely held belief, told the new principal, "This school is failing, and it's your fault!" Meanwhile, the faculty was fractured and hurting and convinced that the school's failure was the fault of the students, whose parents obviously did not share the school's values or support their children in any meaningful way. Teacher turnover was high, and morale was low. For four of the last six years, the district budget had seen no increases, resulting in a significant decline in staff and services at the district and building levels. In short, Beardsley was viewed as a prime example of failed schooling.

Amy Marshall bought none of this. Instead, she recognized that the fate of the school and the future of her kids rested with her and her staff. No magic bullet would fix the school's poisonous reputation or miraculously change the conditions of students' lives. Help from the district, the state, or the federal government? Not likely, when well over half of the district's 30-plus schools fell afoul of NCLB just as steep cuts in revenue were taking place. Not likely, considering Beardsley is located in a state reputed to have one of the largest achievement gaps in the nation but that has failed to provide ailing schools with adequate funding or transformative know-how. Not likely, when the federal government turned the tap on NCLB accountability at the same time it turned its back on the financial commitment needed to sustain transformation.

Not an auspicious start for a success story. Yet it was because of this school's success and the fact that it was named a demonstration school by the National Urban Alliance for Effective Education (NUA) that colleagues from a neighboring state came to Beardsley. Since 2006, NUA has been providing professional development activities for teachers, administrators, and students in several Bridgeport schools, including Beardsley.

Today, Beardsley boasts impressive student gains. Between the 2005–2006 school year—when NUA began its partnership with Beardsley School—and the 2011–2012 school year, the improvement rate of Beardsley students has garnered much attention and recognition. In 2010, the school made Safe Harbor in both math and reading. In this year, 94 percent of Beardsley 6th graders scored at or above proficiency in math, and 85 percent scored at or above proficiency in writing. On the same day as the New York City visit, Beardsley was recognized as a "Success Story School" by the Connecticut Coalition for Achievement Now, a statewide education reform and advocacy group better known as ConnCAN. In May 2011, the school was featured on *Anderson Cooper 360°*, CNN's nightly news broadcast. The feature captured the excitement and power of students learning with their teachers in shared professional learning sessions as well as of students leading professional learning sessions for teachers. The topic? The neuroscience of learning. Their grade levels? Fifth and 6th grade. In 2012, the school was awarded the National School Change Award by the National Principals Leadership Institute. Beardsley is one of six schools to win this award and the only elementary school in the group.

Beardsley School is well on its way to becoming an oasis of success, a school with a clear vision and a renewed culture.

AIMing to Become an Oasis of Success

As we discussed in the introduction, this book lays out three routes to transformation: affirmation, inspiration, and mediation. When taken together, the initials of these routes spell out *AIM*, an acronym we have adopted to describe how these three actions enable schools to foster self-directed learning and self-actualization.

We have purposely borrowed the acronym *AIM* from a special program we have encountered that is designed for those lucky enough to be labeled gifted. The implications of the name bothered us. If one set of students is in the AIM program, does that mean that the remaining students are in the aimLESS program?

This choice of words signifies the ways in which "the haves" continue to receive institutional gifts for which they do not have a particular birthright. These students and their learning are routinely affirmed, inspired, and mediated. School-dependent students, on the other hand, are often accused rather than affirmed ("It is their fault scores are low"); denigrated rather than inspired ("What can you expect from this population?"); and deprived rather than mediated ("Let's give them a dumbed-down curriculum they can handle") (Jackson, 2011).

As we looked more closely at fearless leaders, we discovered that a key to their success involved using the AIM values to guide every aspect of school decision making. These values were applied to everyone, not just a chosen few. We believe that real transformation requires a radical shift in focus that ruptures existing expectations and rallies *all* students and teachers around the goal of aiming for high intellectual performances.

Before embarking on a journey to instill a new set of values throughout the entire school, leaders need to understand the essential elements, specific manifestations, and unique merits of these values. Although we discuss each in depth in subsequent chapters, the following descriptions provide an overview of what is to come.

Affirmation

Affirmations arise from the recognition of the innate worth of human beings. They acknowledge and remind us of our value, and, in so doing, work miracles on the psyche, unleash latent potential, and cultivate talent that could otherwise languish and atrophy. As a fearless leader, you deeply understand the power of affirmation. You take the time to assess and affirm your own merit. Buoyed by self-understanding, you freely and openly affirm others and deliberately create opportunities for students and staff members to affirm themselves and one another.

In schools where affirmation is firmly entrenched, students routinely applaud one another's efforts without being prompted, teachers and students proudly display and discuss their own strengths, and individual and group accomplishments are acknowledged and broadcast.

Chapter 4 discusses the importance of affirmation to fearless leadership and addresses how you and your leadership team can harness the power of affirmation to respond to a call to action and create a call to action that inspires others to follow.

Inspiration

While affirmation serves as a reminder of self-worth, inspiration provides the energy that drives change. Inspiration paints a portrait of what is possible. It is the suggestive spark that fires up our courage to try something new, to take a risk, to hurl ourselves into places we never believed we could go. Inspiring leaders dig deeply into the wellspring of their core beliefs and attitudes, put them on display for others to see, and maintain unwavering confidence that others will emulate those beliefs and attitudes. Others, in turn, depend on inspiring leaders to provide the thrust that will propel them toward new vistas.

Leaders who inspire drive others to consider possibilities. They organize their schools to support the goal of continuous learning, putting in place such structures as study groups, peer-to-peer learning, examination of student work, and faculty meetings devoted to learning and teaching (otherwise known as "administrivia-free zones").

Chapter 5 explores the wellspring from which fearless leaders draw to inspire others and answers two fundamental questions: What is it that fearless leaders want? And how do they inspire others to share their aspirations?

Mediation

As a fearless leader, you not only affirm and inspire but also mediate. Like affirmation and inspiration, mediation springs from positive beliefs about potential. Mediation is the means, the support, and the deliberate and targeted intervention and structure that enable transformation (Feuerstein, Feuerstein, & Falik, 2010). Mediation shreds the cloak of resistance that often stymies change efforts and replaces it with a sense of trust that someone is there to catch you if you fall.

Mediators are outwardly focused, inserting themselves between others and the desired state. In some instances, mediation translates to amassing the resources that enable others to achieve. In other instances, mediators facilitate interactions to expand understanding and develop the capabilities of students and teachers.

Whether your interest is in mediating individuals, groups of individuals, or an entire institution, you have a desired state in mind (reaching one's highest potential), a variety of means to get there, and a quiet confidence in your ability to assist others in the process of growth and change. Chapters 6 and 7 explore what fearless leaders understand about students' and teachers' needs, and how they use this understanding to propel schools to become oases of success.

Traveling Companions: Who Should Come Along on the Journey?

What was principal Amy Marshall's role in the transformation of Beardsley? Although Marshall herself will tell you the transformation had little to do with her, the literature says otherwise. According to an extensive five-year leadership study conducted by the Wallace Foundation (Louis, Leithwood, Wahlstrom, & Anderson, 2010), leadership matters. It has the second-most profound influence on student achievement (after classroom instruction). Further, where the needs are highest, leadership's effect is greatest.

We believe that the journey to transform an underperforming school into an oasis of success involves multiple participants. As a result, it requires a leader—usually a principal—fearless enough to engage these multiple partici-pants in examining and altering the beliefs, practices, structures, and outcomes that make up the life of the school. In the following two sections, we discuss the roles of these participants—teachers, students, families, and communities—in the transformation journey.

Teacher and Student Leaders

There are many definitions and conceptualizations of leadership. When we talk about fearless leadership, we are referring to the shared leadership of a per-son at the helm with a strong set of beliefs, skills, and dispositions who mines the strengths of others to direct the most meaningful aspects of school life: the instructional program focused on learning and high intellectual performances, the relationships that build cohesiveness and a sense of belonging, and the organizational structures that enable learning and relationships to thrive.

Shared leadership is not universally embraced. Several reports indicate that there is little correlation between distributed or shared leadership in schools and student outcomes (Leithwood, Day, Sammons, Harris, & Hopkins, 2006). However, our experience indicates that shared leadership helps ameliorate the strong sense of disengagement felt by many teachers in urban schools. This disengagement exerts a powerful influence on school culture, classroom climate, and student outcomes. Teachers in urban schools are twice as likely to report dissatisfaction with teaching as are teachers in suburban or rural schools. As the percentage of students from low-income families rises, the level of teacher satisfaction decreases (MetLife, 2011). Yet teachers who have frequent and satisfying interactions with administrators report higher job satisfaction. We have found that when urban leaders affirm teachers' commitment, effort, and loyalty, they create stability, foster program cohesiveness, and bring consistency to the chaos of wildly mixed expectations, values, and beliefs.

We have also witnessed the power of deliberate, authentic, and consistent inclusion of students in the transformation process, and we are convinced that without amplification of student voice, urban schools will continue to wear out teachers and lose students. Fearless leaders orchestrate meaningful ways to increase student participation in key functions of school life, especially in the instructional program. We offer a more detailed explanation of how you can amplify student voice in Chapters 6 and 7.

Families and Community

Schools exist in complicated webs of communities and families. As our chief of staff Ahmes Askia says, "Families do not send us some of their children and leave their best children at home." Families send us the children they have, believing that we will provide them with what they need to succeed (Jackson, 2011).

Fearless leaders foster relationships between the school and the community. Families and communities have a vested interest in what happens in schools. If they are ignored, made to feel unwelcome, or otherwise left out of the life of the school, families and communities are repelled, drawing their own conclusions and often badmouthing teachers and administrators. Communicating with and involving family and community members, on the other hand, breeds understanding and trust and often leads to community advocacy for teachers and administrators. Community strife over issues as contentious as school closings can be minimized with concerted communication efforts (DeWitt & Moccia, 2011) and by engaging families and the community as equal partners in a common cause: helping students to reach their potential.

Common sense, national policy, and local legislation all support creating ties among school, family, and community. Students, families, and communities benefit from engagement efforts that invite authentic conversations, shatter assumptions, and create avenues for sharing strategies and concerns (Henderson, Carson, Avallone, & Whipple, 2011).

Reaching out to the community reflects how school staff members view students. Those who view students solely as charges to be instructed erect an impenetrable wall between the aspirations, values, and culture of families and the community and the education of its children. Those who view students as children with hopes, innate intelligence, and motivation to learn recognize the value of partnering with families and the community to determine how best to foster children's development (Epstein, 1995). The cultural divide between urban educators and urban residents is widening with the ever-increasing influx of immigrant families, who tend to cluster in concentrated pockets of communities. Fearless leaders tap into the community as a leadership resource.

Fearlessly leading an underperforming school toward high intellectual performances does not happen by chance. The good news is that fearlessness can be cultivated. One of the first places to start is to reflect with your leadership team on your school culture, looking for signs of fearlessness and signs of elements that increase fearfulness—what we call power leaks.

Points of Interest: Fearlessness Versus Power Leaks

In our work with schools throughout the United States, we have discerned three vital signs of fearlessness and three corresponding danger signs of power leaks. Figure 1.1 summarizes these signs.

Figure 1.1
The Signs of Fearlessness and Power Leaks

The Vital Signs of Fearlessness	The Danger Signs of Power Leaks
Radically confident	Letting go of hope
Radically present	Capitulating to how others define us
Radically strategic	Ignoring our personal compass

In this context, *radical* means being an agent of change, as opposed to remaining on the periphery and supporting the status quo.

Fearless leaders are radical. The word *radical* has several shades of meaning. On the one hand, it means getting to the root of things with thoroughness. It can also refer to an agent that is likely to take part in a chemical reaction. We use the word in both senses. Fearless leaders get to the root of what matters, and they are integral in sparking and maintaining the change process. Because they are well grounded in sound belief systems that celebrate strengths and cultivate potential, they build others' confidence, and that confidence in turn supports them, even when they are racked by the self-doubt that plagues all of us (Jackson, 2011). Fearless leaders need the self-confidence and courage that allows them to reach out to others. They are acutely aware that transformation is not a one-person performance—that they must take aim at their goals not as lone heroes but as part of a unified effort. They realize that their role is to be present—to show up for students, staff, and community—and then to get out of the way to allow students, staff, and community to take up the challenge. They make the structural and institutional arrangements that promote risk taking and alter the culture of the school. Fearless leaders are strategic. They pick their battles, cognizant of the uniqueness of their school milieu. They cultivate what is present, with the belief that the keys to change are theirs for the taking if they work hard enough to find them.

Fearless leaders recognize the danger signs of power leaks. Power leaks strip a school of its spirit, its resilience, and its potential. Fearless leaders keep hope alive: their own, their students', their teachers', and their community's. Hopelessness ravages the soul and paralyzes the psyche. Where there is hope, there is belief. Where there is belief, there is confidence. Where there is confidence, there is ownership of self. Where there is ownership of self, there is strength and drive to transform a school.

Fearless leaders fight back against those who terrorize their schools through delimiting definitions, rank falsehoods, and malicious intentions. Fearless leaders know who they are and what drove them to education in the first place. They possess a tenacious grip on their personal compass, and they use it to guide their decisions, fight for what is right, and marshal the resources to create success out of the resources present (Jackson, 2011).

Preparation and Exploration

Reflection

With another team member, define *fearless leadership* in your own words. Where do you see your school reflected in terms of the vital signs of fearlessness? Share your responses with the entire team.

Call to Action

Consider conducting one or more of the following actions with your leadership team.

Action 1. Working in pairs, list ways in which your school currently involves students, teachers, families, and community members in the life of the school. Think about the nature of each of the activities. Share your list with the leadership team and create a master list that reflects the thoughts of the entire team. What conclusions can you draw about the ways in which students, teachers, families, and community members participate in the life of the school?

Action 2. Consider an issue currently facing your school (for example, rowdy hallway behavior, poor academic performance, or rival student groups). Consider the ways in which your school is addressing the situation. Do you see affirmation or accusation, inspiration or denigration, mediation or deprivation?

Or observe an interaction involving students and adults anywhere in or around the school. Write down what participants say and do. Analyze the interaction. Do you see affirmation or accusation, inspiration or denigration, mediation or deprivation?

Or take a 10-minute walk around the school with a partner. Collect evidence of affirmation, inspiration, or mediation that you observe during your walk. Write down as precisely as you can what you see or hear.

Action 3. As a team, discuss the following quotation from George Dei in the context of this chapter and consider how it pertains to your school: "Diversity and difference mean a wealth of knowledge is available for the benefit of all. Consequently, schooling and education must proceed from the understanding that everyone in school has something to offer, and that diverse viewpoints, experiences, and perspectives should be heard and valued."

2

To What Are Fearless Leaders Committed?

Travel is fatal to prejudice, bigotry, and narrow-mindedness.

—Mark Twain

Key Considerations

- What is the learning destination of fearless leaders?
- What is the relationship among fearless leading, fearless teaching, and fearless learning?
- What are the five areas of focus that foster transformation?
- What is the relationship between affirmation, inspiration, and mediation and the seven high operational practices of the Pedagogy of Confidence?

Destination: High Intellectual Performances

To be fearless in the current landscape of urban education requires leaders to be grounded by a few key dispositions as they plunge into the heavy lifting required to recognize, reculture, and rekindle schools sagging under the weight of sanctions, initiative overload, and deflated self-image. In districts we have partnered with around the country, we have witnessed the depth and breadth of transformation that takes place when leaders of urban schools shun the stereotypes associated with their students and teachers and single-mindedly focus on one target: high intellectual performances that lead to self-directed learning and self-actualization for all (Jackson, 2011). To achieve high intellectual performances requires a complete culture shift, one that fearless leaders relish spearheading and work assiduously to achieve. Fearless leaders know that simply reaching minimum competency does a profound disservice to their students, whose untapped potential deserves to be cultivated.

Reaching High Intellectual Performances Through Fearless Learning and Fearless Teaching

Affirmation, inspiration, and mediation cannot stop at the office door. They need to be the overarching conditions and value systems that undergird pedagogical practices in every classroom and that guide ways of doing things in every aspect of school life. Only then can they become deeply rooted and enable every student's learning to reach fruition. Fearless leadership is designed to support what really matters in school: fearless learning, fueled by fearless teaching.

The relationship among leadership, learning, and teaching is reciprocal. Fearless leadership fuels teacher confidence and competence, which in turn enable teachers to elicit high intellectual performances from all students. When learning transcends the boundaries of low expectations, students demand more from their teachers, their teachers demand more from their leaders, and schools are propelled into new, uncharted territories of learning and teaching (Jackson, 2011).

Radical Instructional Improvement

The literature (Cooper, 2004; Sanders & Rivers, 1996) is clear on the role of teachers in the learning process: teachers exert a powerful influence on student achievement. Because student motivation is directly related to teachers' confidence, our efforts focus on cultivating fearless teachers who are steeped in the beliefs and practices of what we call the *Pedagogy of Confidence*. The Pedagogy of Confidence is the artful use of the science of learning to elicit high intellectual performances and to motivate self-directed learning and self-actualization in *all* students. It is fueled by three fundamental beliefs about learning:

- Intelligence is modifiable.
- All students benefit from a focus on high intellectual performances.
- Learning is influenced by the interaction of culture, language, and cognition.

The Pedagogy of Confidence empowers and supports students and teachers as they fearlessly pursue demonstrations of high intellectual performances. The Pedagogy of Confidence equips teachers with an unshakable belief in their students' capacity to achieve at high levels as well as the confidence in their own ability to implement the strategies and skills needed to help students to reach these high levels (Jackson, 2011).

The Pedagogy of Confidence AIMs for Success

Leaders committed to the Pedagogy of Confidence build their professional learning, reflection, and feedback activities around five areas of school life that foster transformation:

- High intellectual performances.
- Climate for learning.
- Student motivation and engagement.
- Culturally responsive teaching.
- Student self-directed learning.

Although listed as separate elements, the five areas are highly interrelated. For example, schools that identify culturally responsive teaching as a high-priority area of focus soon discover that attention to this area has a spillover effect. As teachers design lessons that use materials and methods relevant and meaningful to their students, engagement and motivation increase, and the climate for learning grows more positive, which leads students to become increasingly self-directed learners capable of demonstrating high intellectual performances.

The challenge, of course, is how schools go about addressing these focus areas. The Pedagogy of Confidence identifies seven "high operational practices" that, when implemented faithfully and universally, transform classrooms and schools. These high operational practices that support high intellectual performances include

- Identifying and activating student strengths.
- Building relationships.
- Amplifying student voice.
- Eliciting high intellectual performances.
- Providing enrichment.
- Integrating prerequisites for academic learning.
- Situating learning in the lives of students. (Jackson, 2011)

The seven practices work in conjunction to create a new landscape for learning. When we partner with schools, we demonstrate low-effort, high-impact strategies (Jackson, 2011) that enable the schools to implement these high operational practices and provide leaders with the tools to support the practices. We expand on the seven high operational practices in Chapters 6 and 7.

The Relationship Between Values and Practices

One of the major challenges faced by leaders is the challenge of cohesiveness. How do leaders help their school communities understand the relationships among the various aspects of a pedagogical approach, philosophy of learning, and value system? With the Pedagogy of Confidence, alignment is simple. Each of the seven high operational practices of the Pedagogy of Confidence aligns with one of the three values that guide school transformation: affirmation, inspiration, and mediation. Figure 2.1 maps that alignment.

Fearless leaders are committed leaders. To create an oasis of success, they need to make three commitments:

Figure 2.1
The Relationship Between Values and Practices

Leadership Values	High Operational Practices
Teachers employ *affirmation* when they . . .	Identify and activate student strengths. Build relationships. Amplify student voice.
Teachers employ *inspiration* when they . . .	Elicit high intellectual performances. Provide enrichment.
Teachers employ *mediation* when they . . .	Provide prerequisites for academic learning. Situate learning in the lives of students.

• Commitment to an idea: high intellectual performances for all.

• Commitment to cultivating a productive means of achieving high intellectual performances: the Pedagogy of Confidence.

• Commitment to uncovering the connections among the beliefs, practices, structures, and outcomes that coexist in schools.

Preparation and Exploration

Reflection

With another team member, define *high intellectual performances* in your own words. Where do you see your school reflected in terms of high intellectual performances? Share your responses with the entire team.

Call to Action

Consider conducting one or more of the following actions with your leadership team.

Action 1. Examine in detail one of the five focus areas of the Pedagogy of Confidence: high intellectual performances, climate for learning, student motivation and engagement, culturally responsive teaching, and student self-directed learning.

1. In pairs, describe what that element might look like in a classroom if implemented at three different levels: high, medium, and low.

2. Individually, determine where you think your school is in terms of implementing that element. Is your school at a high, medium, or low level of implementation?

3. Share your responses with the rest of the leadership team.

4. Discuss what surprised you, the discoveries you made, and the implications of these discoveries.

Action 2. Review one or two of the seven high operational practices of the Pedagogy of Confidence: identifying and activating student strengths, building relationships, amplifying student voice, eliciting high intellectual performances, providing enrichment experiences, providing prerequisites for academic learning, and situating learning in the lives of students.

1. In pairs, create a list of what you might see in a classroom that would indicate evidence of the practice or practices.

2. Determine where you think your school is in terms of implementing this practice. Is your school at a high, medium, or low level of implementation?

3. Share your list and your assessment with the rest of the leadership team.

4. Discuss what surprised you, the discoveries you made, and the implications of these discoveries.

Action 3. As a team, discuss the following quotation (source unknown) in the context of this chapter and consider how it pertains to your school: "Fearlessness is a way of believing, seeing, being, and doing."

3

Why Fearless Leaders Are Needed:
A Call to Action

> All that is necessary for the triumph of evil is that good men do nothing.
>
> —*Attributed to Edmund Burke*

Key Considerations

- What does it mean to respond to a call to action and to create a call to action that inspires others to respond?
- Why must fearless leaders reconceive their role to enable school transformation?
- What are the critical issues that impinge on urban schools, and what fearless actions can you take to counter them?

The Current Landscape

Many of the major realities affecting urban schools today are embedded in caustic factors imposed on schools from the outside. First, urban students wrestle daily with issues that stem from being forced to live life on the margins of society, both inside and outside school. Second, urban schools have been profoundly influenced by a series of policy decisions—most notably, zero-tolerance policies and NCLB—that have sucked the joy out of schooling. Third, public schools are routinely misrepresented by the media and by others poised to gain from the demise of public schools. Taken together, these factors have reduced many urban schools to fear-saturated environments. As a fearless leader, you are well versed in the reality of your students' lives, the negative impact of key policies, the purposeful misrepresentation of facts, and the role of fear in urban schools (Jackson, 2011)—and you fearlessly articulate the effect of these factors on learning.

A Call to Action

At some point, when we educators weren't paying attention, the conversation about education was coopted and stolen from us. Although we let this happen, we can still do something about it. We can wrestle back a conversation that should be led by those most intimately connected to the public education system: the students who attend an institution originally founded on high-minded principles, and the educators who have chosen to serve these principles and their students.

This chapter is a call to action. A *call to action* is a term borrowed from the world of advertising. Generally made up of two parts, an advertisement contains a message and a call to action—an exhortation to respond *now*. The message frames why the advertised product, service, or way of doing things is crucial to one's well-being or image or to some unfulfilled need. The call to action creates a sense of urgency that gets the reader, viewer, or listener to act—to run to the phone, the local store, or a particular website.

Successful ad campaigns are well thought out, targeted, and attention getting. Not all of them seek commercial gain. Think of the successful campaigns in recent years to ban smoking in public places and to use designated drivers when drinking. When these campaigns were conceived, what they were calling for appeared impossible. Fight big tobacco companies? Change ingrained habits? Alter the way people socialize? Nevertheless, a small group of people recognized the great health and social risks these behaviors engendered, did their research, separated myth from reality, crafted their message, banded together, and took action. They were fearless, and, in the end, they succeeded.

We wrote this chapter to convince you that you, too, can address the issues that prevent urban schools from succeeding. But first, we explore why you should be at the forefront of this effort and how you can start uncovering the fearlessness within your school.

Deciding to Act

The Privileges of Leadership

Two of the privileges of leadership are influence and access to information. Leaders have a choice: they can use these privileges for good, or they can do nothing. As a fearless leader, you believe that with privilege come responsibility and obligation. Therefore, you opt for action. You use information and influence to effectively, tirelessly, and strategically identify the obstacles that keep your school from succeeding.

Revitalizing Leaders

The challenges faced by urban school leaders are daunting. Effectively dealing with these challenges requires a distinct type of leadership, one that revitalizes your internal state while at the same time inspiring the lives of students and teachers.

Most educational leaders base their actions on a common set of values that fall into four general categories: basic human values, general moral values, professional values, and social and political values (Leithwood et al., 2006). However, leaders do not always have the opportunity to translate their values into action. The fewer organizational impediments and policy constraints there are, the better the chances that leaders' values will influence their actions (Hambrick & Brandon, 1988). If you are a leader in a school persistently labeled as underperforming, you undoubtedly face a number of outside impositions that hamper your ability to be guided by your values. Directives from the state and federal governments, as well as local initiatives, occupy valuable time. In many instances, these initiatives come with hand-tying regulations and hand-holding consultants and advisors, all of whom purport to know how to address what is ailing your school. You may feel like many leaders in this position: helpless and stymied in your attempts to bridge the disconnect between the things you value and the unfair conditions your students live in.

As a result, you must jettison tired conceptions of leadership that work in less-challenging environments in favor of conceptions that provide your leadership team with power, vision, insight, and agency.

The Leadership Compass

A compass is an essential traveling tool, especially when one is heading into uncharted territory. From our earliest days as a species, humans have used various forms of compasses as navigational aids.

Fearless leaders possess highly refined internal compasses. They focus intently on a goal, their true north. All their attention is concentrated on this personal direction. But unless everyone else is headed in the same direction, the school will suffer from divergent goals, inconsistent pedagogy, and conflicting values. We often use the following exercise in staff development sessions to illustrate this divergence.

Fearless Leadership: Professional Learning at a Glance

We ask workshop participants to stand up, close their eyes, turn around, and, without opening their eyes, point north. Invariably, when they open their eyes, they see everyone pointing in different directions. The participants repeat the exercise after someone identifies where north actually is, and the results are staggeringly different: everyone is pointing in the same direction. The message is clear. Schools that have not clearly identified a goal will find people going every which way. It is much easier to orient a group of people when the direction is clear to everyone.

A compass contains a magnetized needle that moves in response to changing conditions but always ends up pointing north. Like the needle in the compass, you also need to be able to adjust and reorient yourself responsively, ignoring the many distractions and competing priorities that fill your day.

Reorienting Leadership: Adopting a Nurturing Stance

Navigating toward success using affirmation, inspiration, and mediation is a tricky business, and the way leaders orient themselves to this task is crucial. When we say "orient," we are talking about how leaders point toward what they value and how they define themselves. How you define yourself as a leader influences both how you act and how you react.

In particular, fearless leaders exercise *character orientation*. Like actors, they play a role—or, more often, several roles. According to Aristotle, *character* refers to the quality of a person in a story and can be uncovered by examining that person's reactions to other characters as they play out their roles in a variety of situations. In Aristotle's conception, character has a moral or ethical dimension. In Latin, the word *character* means an engraved or branded mark.

Similarly, the way your leadership team orients itself leaves a mark on your school. The stances you adopt and the metaphors you use to label them reveal important information about your team's moral and ethical dispositions and strongly influence perceptions, actions, and relationships in your school (Lackoff & Johnson, 2003). As a leader, you need to adopt empowering stances that enable you to respond resourcefully to the issues you confront.

The four metaphorical leadership stances we discuss in our introduction—architect, soul friend, muse, and minister—radically transform how schools operate. These stances dramatically affirm others and alter power relationships in schools. Taken as a whole, these stances are nurturing stances, by nature protective, supportive, and encouraging. They are designed and oriented to foster growth and development in others. In the following sections, we outline each of these nurturing stances.

The Fearless Leader as Architect

As architects, fearless leaders create the infrastructure in which schools operate. When you take the stance of an architect, you act as a creative visionary with technical skills. You make use of the resources present in your environment to create a structure uniquely suited to your school's particular set of circumstances and conditions.

Although they are charged with the planning, design, and oversight of projects, architects never work in isolation but with a team of experts, each of whom brings crucial skills and understanding to the design process. Building surveyors, drafters, interior designers, and engineers of various kinds all lend their expertise to the architect's overall concept.

Fearless leaders are willing to be the architects of the school environment and to tackle the thorny issues necessary for renovation and renewal. They are also delighted to invite the expertise of others to ensure a sound, well-informed, and sustainable design. If, as Martin Luther King Jr. reminds us, "We must build dikes to hold back the flood of fear," then it falls to fearless leaders to design dikes strong enough to do the job in urban schools.

The Fearless Leader as Soul Friend

Soul friends have the gift of insight and intuitively grasp cause-and-effect relationships and the inner nature of people and situations. Their acute observational and intuitive skills enable them to make deductions, discern connections and nuances, and perceive subtleties that others easily miss.

Because soul friends know themselves and others well, they are uniquely positioned to cultivate belonging. They build relationships, bridge cultural divides, and uncover inner drives and ambitions. Because friendship is built on mutual interests, values, trust, and support—not on hierarchical or power arrangements—soul friends receive as much as they give.

As a soul friend, you understand the culture of your school, your students, your teachers and colleagues, and your community. You engage others in recognizing their self-worth and their potential.

In Hebrew, the term for education is translated as "early rain," a description that conjures images of seeds awakening and responding to the gentle touch of life-giving rain to bud, grow, and reach fruition. Soul friends are the "early rain on a thirsty soul" (J. McDermott, personal communication, 2011) that nourishes and awakens the dormant potential of others.

The Fearless Leader as Muse

Throughout history, muses have been associated with knowledge and the arts. Muses unblock stuck writers, turn on the tap of creativity, and support artists willing to take a risk. In literature, the muse is often thought of as the true speaker, while the author is simply the mouthpiece.

As a fearless leader who takes the stance of muse, you are the "true speaker" who provides the impetus, the inspiration, and the sustenance that allow members of your school to find their own way and to flourish. Like the muse of mythology, you inspire students and teachers to leap into learning and allow themselves to excel. "Mission accomplished" is not part of the muse's vocabulary; continually moving to the next desired state is.

The Fearless Leader as Minister

As minister, the fearless leader's role is to support others. To minister is actually the root of the word *administrator*, and the fearless leader takes this meaning to heart. In the stance of minister, you attend to the needs of others, providing care and renewing the spirit. Your ego is nowhere to be seen. Instead, you look for opportunities to bring out the best in your students, staff, and colleagues. You celebrate others' successes. You redirect them with loving understanding when they go astray. You provide comfort, solace, and respite, often by tapping into resources, advocating on behalf of others, building on people's strengths, and acting as an intermediary to enable others to achieve their potential.

Fearless Leadership as a Calling

Architects, soul friends, muses, and ministers share common perspectives and goals. Each is outwardly oriented and dedicated to clearing the way for others to find their paths. These roles are supportive, as opposed to directive. They recognize that each school's journey to success is different, as each school adapts to its unique circumstances, develops its unique strengths, and finds its unique route.

Connecting Leadership Values and Nurturing Stances

In a school that intends to incorporate the values of affirmation, inspiration, and mediation as crucial design and governing elements, leadership orientation and behaviors must mirror and enhance these values. Figures 3.1 and

Figure 3.1
Connections Between Leadership Values and Nurturing Stances

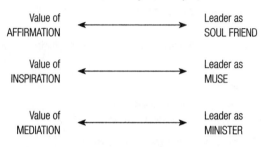

Leader as ARCHITECT:

Creates the superstructure that blends
essential values with key leadership stances.

Value of AFFIRMATION	←———————→	Leader as SOUL FRIEND
Value of INSPIRATION	←———————→	Leader as MUSE
Value of MEDIATION	←———————→	Leader as MINISTER

3.2 illustrate the connections between the leadership values and the leadership stances we have laid out.

Fearless leaders engage others. As an architect, you engage team support. As a soul friend, you engage spirit. As a muse, you engage the mind. As a minister, you engage resources. As all of these, you energize your school, affirming the school community's combined wisdom, good intentions, and desire for success.

Snapshot: Bulletin Boards and High Intellectual Performances

One day, a group of teachers from a number of different schools in the same district were discussing an announcement of administrator transfers. Their comments made clear which leaders were doers, and which were not; which leaders focused on what mattered, and which did not; and which leaders were forces for change, and which were not. One particularly telling conversation centered on bulletin boards. The district had recently launched an initiative to use bulletin boards to demonstrate current student work tied to standards, and to date the

Figure 3.2
Behaviors Associated with Leadership Stances and Nurturing Values

The leader as ARCHITECT creates the superstructure, or frame, that blends fearless values with fearless stances.

The value of AFFIRMATION mirrors the leadership stance of SOUL FRIEND.
- Affirmation arises from positive assumptions about the innate worth of others.
- Soul friends get to the heart of what matters to the other person.
- Soul friends and affirmation derive from the same set of underlying principles: belief, trust, and support.

The value of INSPIRATION mirrors the leadership stance of MUSE.
- Inspiration propels creative invention.
- Muses urge others to go beyond their self-imposed limits.
- Muses and inspiration spring from promise and possibility.

The value of MEDIATION mirrors the leadership stance of MINISTER.
- Mediation is a support mechanism.
- Ministers intervene on behalf of others.
- Ministers and mediation are the springboards for achievement.

content on the boards. One group of teachers told another, "Don't worry about your new principal. He rarely leaves his office. When it comes to bulletin boards, just change the date every few months, and you'll be OK. He never actually looks at the content of the bulletin boards; he just checks the date." The principal under discussion did not AIM for success. He displayed none of the characteristics of fearlessness and failed to take any of the four nurturing stances.

Fortunately, during the same conversation, discussion shifted to several principals who were universally admired. As one teacher put it, her principal "restored belief and pride" in the school, "made me a better teacher," and "makes everyone feel that we have important work to do, and somehow, we do it." When pressed for more details, she explained how the principal had turned the district-imposed bulletin board initiative into an exciting learning and community-building experience that dovetailed with the learning and teaching goals of the school, far surpassing the district's goal of merely displaying student work.

The school's faculty had previously identified high intellectual performances as a learning goal, and professional learning opportunities focusing on this goal were part of the life of the school. Rather than railing against the imposition of the bulletin board initiative, the principal encouraged the faculty to discuss how the initiative could support their goal. From this discussion, a plan emerged: every time a class was ready to display a new bulletin board, a High Intellectual Performances Bulletin would be sent out to all students and teachers. During an unveiling ceremony designed and implemented by students, the class members would explain what they had learned, how they had learned it, and how their learning demonstrated high intellectual performances. Students and teachers from visiting classes would provide verbal and written affirmations. Visitors to the school who happened upon the hallway exhibits also had a chance to leave affirmations. Each display included an envelope full of sticky notes and markers that invited visitors to take part in sharing affirmations. Teachers volunteered to conduct explorations of their pedagogy that provided opportunities for their colleagues to affirm their efforts, provide feedback, and discuss possible enhancements.

Students and teachers loved the steady stream of accolades their work engendered (affirmation); tried to "outdo" one another in a friendly spirit of competition during these public displays of learning and teaching (inspiration); and learned from one another (mediation). These outcomes are the products of fearless leading. This is a principal who affirmed, inspired, and mediated through a combination of the stances of architect, soul friend, muse, and minister. She responded to a call to action and, in turn, led a call to action.

Setting Off on the Journey

The two principals described above represent two visions of leadership: one passive, the other active. One is strangled by fear and mired in immobility. The other is emboldened, inventive, and on the move.

Fearless leaders are unflinching in the wake of overwhelming odds. They are leading the transformation of their schools into oases of success. Like you, their first steps on this road involve affirmation, inspiration, and mediation.

Affirmation: Acknowledge Realities

As a fearless leader, you understand the big picture. You do not shy away from or minimize harsh realities. Instead, you acknowledge and affirm the lives lived by your students and teachers. You understand that stakes are high for your students and for the nation as a whole. You understand that you have the power to present a different take on what is really going on in your school. You possess great insight into what can be done to address the many challenges your school faces in large and small ways every day. You have the gumption to fight back against the media and the anti–public education movement that have powerfully influenced the national discourse about public education.

Inspiration: Take a Leap of Faith

Charting a new course means letting go of the comfortable, stepping off the worn path—and taking a leap of faith.

Fearless Leadership: Professional Learning at a Glance

We often begin our leadership development sessions by showing a series of images that depict four different scenes. We ask participants to select the one that best represents their lives as leaders in urban schools. One photograph shows a train crossing a deep ravine on a breathtakingly high bridge. Another is of a series of hands intertwined to form a face with its tongue sticking out. A third depicts an ancient statue leaning over with its hand cupped over its ear, as if trying to listen in on the cell-phone conversation of a museum visitor walking by. The last image—the one that routinely gets the biggest response—shows a person standing on the edge of a very high mountain ready to zip-line across to the other side. Participants often say that they feel they are always on the edge, poised for a scary ride over a seemingly bottomless ravine.

Leading an urban school today is not unlike zip-lining, skydiving, or bungee jumping. What all these activities have in common is that they require specialized equipment, a dedicated and well-trained support team, and a person with the internal drive and fortitude—the gumption—to take the first bold step off the cliff, out the airplane door, or into the abyss. All of these activities require fearlessness.

Those who fearlessly take this bold step have one other key ingredient: faith. Although you may not know what you will find at the other end of this step, you know that you cannot stay where you are—perched and tense and shackled by fear. You have faith that, as scary as it may be, taking that step will get you to the other side.

In short, your willingness to take a leap of faith and plunge headlong into the work of transformation is inspirational. That first step is often all that is needed to spark a movement.

Mediation: Build Buy-In

As a fearless leader, you enlist the buy-in of others by intentionally opening up avenues for constituent participation in defining and resolving issues. You recognize that no single "truth" captures what is happening in your school. Instead, you understand that the way each person sees the school experience and understands what is required for improvement needs to be part of any discussion of school transformation.

Naturally, insiders and outsiders perceive images and events differently. Further, the "official" story of record or defining image is frequently limited by the vantage point of the narrator, whose own experiences drive his or her choices about what to include and what to exclude (Sontag, 2003). Sontag illuminates the dangers inherent in the effort to narrate the lives and experiences of others, referring to Virginia Woolf's (1938) observation about the power and variability of perceptions: "The eye is connected with the brain; the brain with the nervous system. That system sends its messages in a flash through every past memory and present feeling." As a fearless leader, you recognize that every encounter in or out of school is mediated by your own culture and experiences. Therefore, you work to amplify the voices of students, teachers, and community members as essential elements in the conversation about the experience of school.

Understanding this, you lead a call to action in the context of openness, the kind that invites and registers the perspectives of those often omitted from conversations about school: community members, teachers, and, especially, students. You understand that without their buy-in, change efforts—no matter how well intentioned and well researched—will be seen as yet another outside imposition designed to "fix" someone else's challenges. You orchestrate ways to uncover common experiences and aspirations. Out of respect, you do not impose the force of your will and position on others. Instead, you act as a mediator who guides others to new understanding. You provide the organizational arrangements and ferret out the necessary resources that open up paths to discussion, understanding, and vision.

Architects of Transformation Revisited

According to renowned architect Frank Lloyd Wright, "Every great architect is—necessarily—a great poet. He must be a great original interpreter of his time, his day, his age." We have found that every fearless urban school leader is an architect. Like poets, fearless leaders see beauty and hope where others see wreckage and dead ends. Fearless leaders embrace the challenges inherent in creating spaces alive with dreams, belonging, and learning. Fearless leaders amass resources and mine strengths. Fearless leaders recognize that leaders have the power to shape how a school does business, from how meetings are run to how people relate to one another.

In the next three chapters, we present how the poet architect interprets "her time, her day, her age" through the innovative, renewing, and efficacious roles of a soul friend who affirms, a muse who inspires, and a minister who mediates.

Points of Interest: Characteristics of Fearless Leaders

• Fearless leaders are optimistic that they can and will succeed. Without optimism, change withers on the vine. Fearless leaders cultivate and model an optimistic stance. Optimistic leaders do not see problems as immutable obstacles impeding their success. Instead, they consider what steps they should take to mitigate the problem.

• Fearless leaders are caring and smart enough to understand the complexity and history of the factors that have contributed to the current state of affairs. Fearless leaders are good listeners who bring up the issues people really want to talk about.

• Fearless leaders are courageous enough to overthrow outdated or unproductive conceptions of schools, school governance, and school mission. *Overthrow* is a strong word, and it takes a strong leader to ask questions that dig deeply into the whys and wherefores of an institution. It takes fearless leaders to question the status quo. Why, fearless leaders might ask, are we giving out "survival kits" to new teachers during orientation? What messages are embedded in this seemingly humorous gesture? What message would we send if we instead gave new teachers a "thriving kit" containing positive messages about how learning and teaching are enacted in this school and school-based resources to help the novice teachers hone their skills?

• Fearless leaders have heard the call to action, and they are ready to take the first step to lead their own call to action. You are the leader your school has been waiting for. As an individual, you are strong. As part of a team, you are an irrepressible force.

Preparation and Exploration

Reflection

With another team member, define *call to action* in your own words. Discuss any indications you see that your school is ready to respond to a call to action. Share your responses with the entire team.

Call to Action

Consider conducting one or more of the following actions with your leadership team.

Action 1. Identify a local issue that negatively affects your students' lives.

• Describe the issue.
• Describe how it affects students' school lives.
• Describe how the school has attempted to address this situation.

Explore some solutions you might come up with through affirmation, inspiration, or mediation.

Action 2. Identify the architects, soul friends, muses, and ministers among the staff in your school. Analyze how each contributes to the life of the school, and discuss specific ways in which their skills can help lead a school to transformation.

Action 3. Identify the architects, soul friends, muses, and ministers among your students and their families. Discuss how your school could tap these resources in a more coordinated, strategic way to contribute to school transformation.

Action 4. As a team, discuss the following quotation from H. G. Wells in the context of this chapter and consider how it pertains to your school: "History is a race between education and catastrophe."

Part 2

The Itinerary

Once a leadership team makes the decision to transform its school into an oasis of success, an important question arises: how do you get there without being sidetracked? The next four chapters describe a recommended itinerary: transformation through affirmation, inspiration, and mediation. These three values have an interesting relationship with one another that we can illuminate through a geographical metaphor.

In Quebec, Canada, two rivers converge just outside Montreal: the Ottawa and St. Lawrence Rivers. Just past this convergence point, the topography changes, and boaters are faced with a major maritime barrier, the Lachine Rapids. Year-round, these powerful rapids hamper safe passage through Montreal.

Historically, the rapids were a major danger point that had to be passed if goods were to be shipped safely and transportation lanes were to be opened to the rest of Canada. In the early 1800s, the Lachine Canal was built to bypass the rapids. As a result, Montreal prospered, hydraulic power was made available for the developing industries along the banks of the canal, and entire neighborhoods sprang up to take advantage of plentiful job opportunities in the factories flanking the canal.

We look at the Ottawa and St. Lawrence Rivers as affirmation and inspiration, with the Lachine Canal acting as mediator. Just as the canal regulates and directs where the waters go, mediation helps channel the energy and movement of your school toward transformation.

Every school is different, and there are multiple starting points and paths toward the desired destination. However, affirmation, inspiration, and mediation are essential routes to take in transforming a school into an oasis of success. In the next four chapters, we focus on these major routes and on the actions that you, as a leader, must take to successfully navigate the choppy waters of transformation.

In each chapter, we discuss the initial lay of the land—the conditions or contexts that define where schools currently stand—and then explain how affirmation, inspiration, or mediation can address these conditions. Along the way, we provide snapshots of these elements in action as well as points of interest that can guide your team in uncovering your current position and charting a course to a new destination.

4

Fearless Leaders as Soul Friends:
Affirmation in Action

> Fearlessness is like a muscle. I know from my own life that the more
> I exercise it, the more natural it becomes to not let my fears run me.
>
> —*Arianna Huffington*

Key Considerations

- What are the outside realities that define and affect urban learners?
- What do fearless leaders who reorient themselves as soul friends recognize and understand?
- What does affirmation mean in the context of leadership and transformation?
- How do soul friends use affirmation to mitigate the negative influence of outside conditions?
- What does affirmation in action look like?
- What steps can leadership teams take to reorient themselves as soul friends and to explore the landscape of affirmation?

Orientation: The Landscape of Urban Education

The Realities of Students' Lives

Those of us who have devoted our lives to public education in the United States' most challenged communities are acutely aware of the realities of students' lives outside school, the resources they have been denied inside school, and the fury that can erupt after years of being treated as expendable, unworthy, and nothing more than a problem (Jackson, 2011). These realities constitute the jumping-off point for change.

The Making of School Dependency

The cumulative effect of these detrimental realities seeps into every crevice of school and creates a new class of students: those considered school-dependent. By *school-dependent,* we mean students who, through no fault of their own, rely heavily on school personnel to ensure that they have the advantages they need to reach their potential, including an environment that acknowledges their merit and the richness of their experiences. School-dependent students are those whose parents are working two or three low-wage jobs and have neither the energy nor the time to help their children with homework. School-dependent students are those whose immigrant parents do not understand the U.S. school system and who themselves have little formal education. School-dependent students are those who suffer from the ongoing racism that unfairly burdens them with the baggage of identity threats and the fear of confirming negative stereotypes (Steele, 2010).

As an urban educator, you know that family and community violence has insidious effects on cognitive processes and emotional well-being (Jackson, 2011; Margolin & Gordis, 2000). In the United States, nearly one-quarter of all children ages 0–17 live in poverty, and these rates are three times higher for African American and Hispanic children than for white children (U.S. Census Bureau, 2009). Forty percent of children living in chronic poverty show "deficiencies in at least two areas of functioning (such as language and emotional responsiveness) at age 3" (Bradley et al., 1994, cited in Jensen, 2009).

You have undoubtedly used your own resources to support students who go to bed hungry at night. You know the challenges faced by immigrant families whose welcome wagon is filled with hostility, distrust, grudgingly administered aid, and denied opportunities. You are painfully aware that some schools specialize in the production of dropouts (Fine, 1991). You are already witnessing what Reuven Feuerstein has identified as a "cognitive holocaust" (personal communication, August 28, 2007) propelled by school-dependent students' lack of access to enrichment and the high operational practices needed to nurture their intellectual potential (Jackson, 2011).

Countless urban schools struggle daily to survive these negative effects. In many suburban and rural schools, the pernicious effects of economic and social gaps similarly take their toll. All these gaps and injustices have been thrown into sharp relief in recent years, thanks to analyses of academic performance that further marginalize and problematize students made to feel school-dependent by segregating them into "subgroups" according to various descriptors, such as race and socioeconomic status.

Left to its own devices, our education system will continue to drive a permanent wedge between the haves and the have-nots. Such a system is destined to implode—and the nation will implode with it. It is in our collective self-interest, then, to acknowledge this situation and modify our actions accordingly. It is up to fearless leaders to craft the message that will communicate what Dr. Martin Luther King Jr. referred to in his "I Have a Dream" speech as the "fierce urgency of now" (1963) and apply it to narrow the race and culture gaps within and across schools, as well as between students and their teachers (Cooper & Jackson, 2011).

To date, solutions to address the myriad ways in which certain students are school-dependent and are made to feel school-dependent have proven elusive.* Even among those who profess to care about the many U.S. students who do not reach their potential, the impulse is to run from the problem, claiming that the contributing factors are too broad to be handled by school personnel, or to throw up their hands in defeat, claiming that students and their families are to blame. But those who take the time to listen to students as they attempt to

---

*What's the difference between "school-dependent" and "made to feel school-dependent"? Many urban students are school-dependent in that they lack enriching supports due to low socioeconomic status; however, students are made to *feel* school-dependent when teachers ignore the skills and strengths they do possess.

Two-Tiered Opportunities: What the Research Says

Recent research has indicated that conditions that provide different opportunities for different social strata have not served the United States well and that if they continue, the results could be catastrophic. A longitudinal study spanning 30 years (Wilkinson & Pickett, 2009) indicates several unsettling trends:

• On almost every measure associated with a healthy society (mental illness, life expectancy and infant mortality rates, homicide rates, imprisonment rates, obesity rates, social mobility, and children's educational performance), the United States compared unfavorably with other countries, developed or not.

• The United States has one of the largest gaps between the rich and everyone else.

• The healthiest and happiest societies are those that have the smallest gaps between rich and poor.

• Unequal societies are bad for everyone within them, whether rich or poor.

In addition to these sobering findings, neuroscientific research on the effects of poverty on learning illustrate how poverty and its attendant risk factors damage the physical, socioeconomic, and cognitive well-being of children and their families. Jensen (2009) explains how chronic socioeconomic deprivation can create environments that undermine the development of self and the capacity for self-determination.

navigate a life strewn with enormous impediments hear dreams, aspirations, and insights that are crying out to be broadcast.

Snapshot: Justice Epistles

For many urban youths, life is hard. Their life narratives include intimate experiences with homelessness, violence, racism, inequality, poverty, and crime. They worry about child labor, abuse, and recruitment into street gangs. They are saddled with thorny concerns and mired in experiences that should have no part in their young lives.

In *The Justice Epistles* (National Urban Alliance for Effective Education & the Newark Public Schools, 2011)—letters to various adults, including parents, teachers, administrators, government officials, and national organizations— middle school students in Newark, New Jersey, express the reality of their life narratives with astuteness and eloquence. Two things stand out as one reads these letters. The first is that such realities exert tremendous physical, emotional, and psychological tolls on these young learners. The second is that these students, like young people everywhere, live in hope that the adults around them will not abandon them to the chaos, destruction, and fear of a world in free fall.

Several particularly moving epistles address the issue of gangs. For the 6th, 7th, and 8th graders who discuss this topic, close experiences with gangs are part of the landscape of their lives, and all have great insight into different aspects of the problem. Traesha recounts the gang killing of someone she knew. She observes, "Putting candles on the street and balloons and stuffed animals has not really helped keep it from happening again." José tells of his flirtation with and eventual submission to the world of gangs, an attraction that began at the age of 9. Although he knew it was wrong, and his family warned him against it, his "knucklehead skull never listened." His account of his dangerous escapades ends with the reflection, "I was living in a music-video world." Kendall, who has had three family members die because of gang-related violence, explains, "Gangs are not only about turf and power and the killings, but the worst thing of all is the drugs." He opines, "I know it's going to get even crazier now that Newark has let so many Newark police officers go to unemployment because of some tax thing which makes no sense to me." It makes no sense to anyone else who cares about these children, either.

We cannot afford to ignore these realities. We need to recognize them as real and present in our students' lives, not only because of the effect they have on students' frames of reference and emotions, but also because of the tremendous adverse effects they have on students' cognitive and goal-setting abilities.

The Justice Epistles demonstrates both the detrimental realities of students' lives and these students' potential, courage, and wisdom. These letters encourage leaders to reorient themselves on behalf of students, to see urban students for who they are, and to experience hope buoyed by a shift in perspective.

Reorientation: Fearless Leaders as Soul Friends Who Affirm

What Do Soul Friends Recognize and Understand?

A *soul friend* is an age-old concept derived from the ancient Celts that refers to a friend, teacher, companion, spiritual guide, or other person to whom one confesses (O'Donohue, 1997). Soul friends build and maintain deep and knowing relationships that allow them to understand and respond to others in deep and powerful ways. Soul friends recognize the hurdles of reality. They also understand that affirmations have the power to step over the wreckage of reality and touch the spirit. Positive affirmations can reprogram negative beliefs, mitigating the effect of disparaging feedback that staff and students receive from the stereotypes, negative influences, and derogatory labels associated with urban schools. Positive affirmations are powerful catalysts for motivating staff and students to set and pursue goals for their success (Jackson, 2011).

Leaders who are committed to reorienting themselves as soul friends recognize five key aspects of their current reality. They understand that

• Student success is directly related to teachers' confidence in their students' intellectual potential and to their ability to elicit that potential (Jackson, 2011).

• Learning and teaching are complex enterprises not easily reduced to simple formulas.

• Learning and teaching are affected by myriad influences and conditions that tap into every facet of life: physical, emotional, cultural, and social.

• The realities of students' lives outside school must be acknowledged as real, true, and present in their lives as learners (Jackson, 2011).

• Fear is a factor in deflating will, stifling vision, and deadening the spirit that enticed educators to go into the field in the first place (Jackson, 2011).

These leaders also recognize three fundamentals about transformation and schools. They understand that

• Major, lasting, transformative societal and personal changes are fueled by changes in beliefs (Feuerstein, 1979; Feuerstein et al., 2010).

• Schools are not values-free zones.

• A school is a community with an identifiable structure, culture, mission, and set of relationships.

These interrelated understandings explain why some schools are "magical places where dreams happen" and "sacred places of possibility and transformation" (Feuerverger, 2007) while others are stultifying environments that suffocate promise. As a soul friend, you cultivate the positive beliefs and optimistic values that renew your school's culture.

Things to See and Do: Transformation Through Affirmation

As a fearless leader who is a soul friend, you nurture affirming beliefs, shift perspective by surfacing and affirming strengths, and recognize the power of affirmations to elicit high intellectual performances from students. By looking more deeply into these three major actions, a picture of why and how affirmation is a catalyst for transformation begins to emerge.

Nurture Affirming Beliefs

Acknowledged or not, beliefs influence every action and reaction in the complex structure we call school. An undeviating through line binds beliefs, practices, structures, and outcomes. If the prevailing belief in your school is that students have learning potential, then your practices will encourage students to pursue intellectually stimulating activities; structures will be in place to give students the independence, resources, and assistance to address complex problems; and students will produce cognitively complex and insightful work. Sadly, the opposite is true when beliefs about students are negative or diminishing.

Embrace positive beliefs. As a soul friend, you believe that your students possess a wealth of untapped strengths and that it is your job to nurture these strengths to fruition. You also believe that all brains seek the same thing: engagement, challenge, reflection, and feedback (Jensen, 2005). You believe that intelligence is modifiable, that all students benefit from a focus on high intellectual performances, and that learning is influenced by the interaction of culture, language, and cognition (Jackson, 2011).

This set of beliefs is transformative. It is based on a set of positive assumptions and suggests potential for growth. It represents a life raft for students and a set of oars for teachers who have been tossed around by wave after wave of negativity, finger pointing, and sanctions. Simply stating these beliefs at an open house, mounting them on classroom bulletin boards, or putting them on letterhead, however, will not change what happens in schools. Stale beliefs do not automatically make way for new beliefs.

Interrogate beliefs. As a soul friend, you guide people to critically interrogate beliefs to demolish walls of "hidden impositions" (M. McDermott, personal communication, 2011). To "critically interrogate" means to cast a long, laser-sharp look at the beliefs that shape our behaviors, whether those beliefs are stated or implied.

Fearless Leadership: Professional Learning at a Glance

We believe that communities are "born and nurtured in webs of conversation" (Garmston & Wellman, 2009). One of the most effective ways to uncover beliefs is by providing structured opportunities to explore and discuss provocative texts (print or multimedia) that tap into the wellspring of our beliefs. These encounters with beliefs can be disconcerting. They take will, effort, planning, and fearlessness. But without surfacing the latent values and attitudes that seep into all aspects of school life, no substantive transformation will occur. This work is best accomplished in settings that are crafted for ease of sharing, openness, and curiosity, such as guided faculty and grade-level meetings, professional learning sessions, or study groups. In our work with schools, we use a variety of text-based discussion strategies and community-enhancing protocols that provide some shelter from the storm that is often unleashed in the wake of these conversations. Communities should take charge of their own learning, and that intentional use of agreed-upon protocols is one way to do so in a safe and trusting environment (McDonald, Mohr, Dichter, & McDonald, 2007).

Cultivate shared beliefs. As your team surfaces and examines individual beliefs, you, as a soul friend, will begin the work of cultivating the shared values that will create the shared culture needed to sustain and energize your school. These values include dedication to nurturing individual strengths in the context of shared commitment and creative curiosity; minimizing power relationships and maximizing opportunities for individual growth and self-direction; and joyfully listening to, learning from, and interacting with one another.

Shift Perspective: Affirm Strengths

Many schools have teams devoted to uncovering what the data say about student performance. What data team, however, spends time examining what students do *well?* Usually, the work of these teams focuses on ferreting out the lowest scores, the poorest areas of performance, and students' pronounced weaknesses—tasks that cannot help but highlight deficits. Deliberately rupturing the deficit model by searching for strengths is a powerful perspective-shifting tool (Jackson, 2011). As a soul friend, you use affirmations to dramatically reshape how students and teachers see themselves and how others see them. You cultivate positive self-image, and, in a departure from the norm, you look for and acknowledge the positive aspects of student and teacher performance and behavior.

Eliminate misplaced personal insecurity. What often prevent school leaders from using their position to influence others are a misplaced sense of insecurity and a cultivated lack of confidence. Leaders are made to feel inadequate to an increasingly complex and impossible task. They suffer from overload, and they feel vulnerable. These feelings foster a destructive dependency on quick fixes, the next big idea in management theories, and other externally imposed solutions (Fullan, 1998). Awareness of personal values and strengths is a potent first step to fearless leadership. Leaders are often painfully unaware of their capacity simply because they rarely have a chance to discuss their values or to enumerate their strengths. It is emancipating when they do so.

Fearless Leadership: Professional Learning at a Glance

When we ask leaders to enumerate the leadership characteristics that are essential to address today's educational challenges, they have no problem identifying them. They assert that leaders need to be

- Courageous.
- Confident.
- Nonjudgmental.
- Enthusiastic.
- Adaptable.
- Tenacious.
- Accessible.
- Consistent.
- Informed.
- Visible.
- Resilient.
- Compassionate.

When asked to highlight their own three strongest characteristics, they do so with relish and insight.

When your leadership team goes through this exercise and shares results, everyone benefits. A robust mosaic forms, and all can readily see how each member contributes something different to the mosaic as a whole while maintaining his or her own uniqueness. This exercise enables your team members to affirm one another's strengths and assign roles according to those strengths. From this cultivated psychological hardiness comes a renewed sense of control and influence, which in turn reignites the energy you need to pursue your purpose and mission.

Taking stock of and affirming positive characteristics yield positive results. Stress, the unwanted but constant companion of urban school leaders, has myriad effects on physical and mental health. Research suggests that self-affirming activities reduce the psychological effects of stress (Creswell et al., 2005). Self-affirmation enables leaders to see themselves as "competent, good, stable, capable of choice and control" (Steele, 1988, p. 289)—all necessary precursors to taking fearless action.

Shift teacher attitudes and expectations of students. As teachers begin to affirm student strengths, their attitudes and expectations shift—and so do their behaviors. This orientation shift is supported by the vast amount of research demonstrating the effect of teacher expectations on student performance (Rist, 2000; Solomon, Battistich, & Hom, 1996). Teachers who free themselves from unexamined biases allow themselves to see the merit, worth, and capacity of their students. Respecting who students are and eliciting demonstrations of their potential is a crucial step to becoming an effective teacher. A by-product of this shift in orientation is the way teachers perceive students who are socially, culturally, or racially different from themselves. They no longer view diversity as a problem but affirm and celebrate it as a valuable resource (Cooper, 2009; Nieto, 1996).

Fearless Leadership: Professional Learning at a Glance

One simple yet powerful method for using affirmations to reshape a school culture is to start the school year with a strengths survey that asks teachers to enumerate their own strengths and to spend the first few weeks of school looking for their students' strengths. The deliberate process of uncovering and naming strengths leads educators to think, "Of course I possess positive values and desirable qualities, and so do my students."

It is also crucial to involve students—especially students of color—in self-discovery and self-affirmation activities. In a recent study (Cohen, Garcia, Apfel, & Master, 2006), a group of researchers from Yale University divided randomly selected African American and white 7th grade students into two groups. Each group was assigned a 15-minute writing exercise: students in the experimental group chose their most important value from a list and explained its importance, while students in the control group wrote about their least important value. African American students in the experimental group received higher grades than their counterparts in the control group and reduced the racial achievement gap by 40 percent.

Shift leadership attitudes and expectations of staff. Leaders in the throes of changing school culture often feel stymied by the staff members who tend to resist change. Fortunately, strategically used relationship- and consensus-building activities can break down the resistance of even the most hardened cynics or frightened traditionalists.

Fearless Leadership: Professional Learning at a Glance

"The Good Fight," a community builder used by NUA, prompts participants to consider this question: "In your professional role, what is the 'thing' you cannot or will not stop fighting for?" Members of the group probe one another for details and provide specific affirmations and encouragement.

A simple 20-minute exercise like this one enables your leadership team to uncover the passions and power of staff members while providing you with insight into common sentiments. There is little room in the protocol for the cynic to sabotage movement forward, nor is the stage so public that the timid educator will be afraid to speak up.

There is a subtle message embedded in this exercise: everyone in the school is on a mission. All are fighting for something, and more often than not, that something is the same for everyone. Participants' affirmation of one another acknowledges that all members of the school possess strengths that enable them to conduct a successful fight for what they believe in. Once the group identifies a common mission, commitment is easy to obtain—often as easy as asking people to fill out a commitment card indicating one thing they will commit to do in the next two weeks in support of the fight.

Students' intellectual life depends profoundly on institutional change. The power of schoolhouse relationships is evident the minute one crosses the threshold of a school. The nature of adult relationships correlates directly to the quality and character of a school and to student performance (Barth, 2006). Improve relationships, then, and student achievement will follow.

Affirming strengths is crucial to sparking a culture shift and awakening a positive group identity among leaders, teachers, and students. As your leadership team surfaces beliefs and shared values, the culture of your school will transform. You will discover your capacity to build relationships and a sense of belonging among formerly fractured, disengaged staff and students. You will bridge cultural divides, engage others in recognizing their self-worth, and insightfully address issues. In the end, these efforts will remake your school.

Recognize the Power of Affirmations

Soul friends are not blind. They see what is happening in the lives of their students and staff, and they address it.

Soul friends turn up the volume on reality checks. In today's world of urban education, fearless leaders need to assert that within urban schools are dedicated teachers and students with vast intellectual capacity, dreams for a brighter future, and the desire to reach their full potential. These teachers and students face challenges that are real and not of their own making. As a soul friend, you recognize the forces that make your students and staff feel "less than," and you cultivate an environment that supports their spirit and empowers them to believe in themselves.

As a soul friend, you work with students and staff to ferret out myths about yourselves and to discuss the issues that negatively affect the undercultivated human capital in your school, who is responsible for addressing these issues, how these issues affect success for everyone, and how the school can counter the effects of the myths and nurture human capital (Jackson, 2011).

Soul friends transform the psychological landscape. Many people who are on the receiving end of a barrage of negative input succumb to the limitations that others impose on them, believing the limitations are in fact a reality (Dweck, 2000). It's your job to break free of these impositions to enable your students and teachers to flourish. You have a responsibility to yourself, your students, your teachers, and the community you serve. As a soul friend, you must begin with positive self-affirmation (which is often the hardest) and then move to affirming others.

On the Road to Transformation

Affirmation Snapshot: Visitacion Valley Middle School

Visitacion Valley Middle School is an island of safety in a sea of trouble, but it was not always that way. In 2004, two students stumbled upon the decomposing body of a 19-year-old stabbing victim—one of many murder victims in this small community on the southern border of San Francisco. Later that same year, a gunman walked into the school, threatened to kill a teacher, and robbed two employees. The school was run like a prison. Lockdowns were frequent, and faculty members were just waiting for the chance to transfer from "the fight school." Visitacion Valley students are no strangers to violence and its after-effects.

The school faces other challenges, as well. Twenty percent of students have an incarcerated parent. And students from Samoa, who make up 15 percent of the student body, find the U.S. education system to be out of touch with their cultural values and norms. For example, they and their families find it difficult to acclimate to a print culture, coming from one steeped in the oral tradition. It is equally difficult for school personnel to adjust to a group of parents who communicate with the school through a sub-chief.

It took a fearless leader—principal James Dierke—to lead the school's transformation. As any soul friend would, Principal Dierke uncovered beliefs, cultivated shared values, and created a new culture. He sought out colleagues who shared his optimism and energy and who possessed strengths that would shore up any he lacked. These key people became his leadership team. In the first two years of his tenure, 20 teachers left—teachers whose beliefs and values did not mesh with the school's new, positive ones. The results speak for themselves: between 2004 and 2010, suspensions dropped precipitously while academic performance improved significantly.

Principal Dierke recognized that if students' and families' basic needs are not met, learning has little chance of blossoming. Through aggressive grant writing and relentless pursuit of community partnerships, the school established a Community Care Team with 26 partners and developed on-site counseling and wellness centers that help make the school a safe and welcoming environment regardless of the issues students and families face. Visitacion Valley also offers various kinds of academic support before and after school, during lunch, and on Saturdays, and the school has introduced clubs that are thriving. Good Will Industries provides job training and résumé-writing services for parents and community members, and the school holds adult literacy classes. In addition, Visitacion Valley is the home of the first on-campus First Tee Golf Center for minority youth in the United States. The First Tee has taught 1,500 students in the community how to play golf while instilling confidence and values such as honesty and integrity. The school even has a dog that "humanizes" the school and is therapeutic for aching souls. The dog goes home every night with one of the teachers, but the students walk the dog during the day.

The leadership team recognized that bridging the cultural divide between the school and its Samoan students was a challenge it needed to take on. Through a concerted effort, the team grew closer to the Samoan community and hired several Samoan paraprofessionals and one Samoan teacher. These individuals help to bridge cultural divides by educating school personnel about Samoan culture, providing familiar cultural touchstones for Samoan students, and educating Samoans about school in the United States. At Principal Dierke's retirement dinner, the Samoan community arrived and made him a Paramount Chief of Sonoma, a very high honor.

Today, Visitacion Valley students and teachers alike are encouraged to recognize their self-worth and to use their talents. Students participate in various activities and contests, and the school has introduced programs like GEAR UP, which sends a message that students *can* go to college. And in a school that used to abstain from off-campus outings because of widespread mistrust of students, students are now valued and responsible citizens, and field trips are part of the fabric of the school.

Teachers are also valued. They lead professional development activities, write grants, and use faculty and grade-level meetings to define pedagogical goals and values. The school provides them with the organizational arrangements and encouragement they need to move their practice to the next level.

When Principal Dierke arrived at Visitacion Valley, his most important challenge was to address the eruptions of violence in the school and their impact on his students' lives. Clearly, the school-as-prison model was not working. Working from the perspective of what students needed to heal and to cope, the school applied for and won a grant from the David Lynch Foundation that provides two 12-minute meditation sessions each day—one at the beginning and one at the end of the school day. Every student and teacher receives personal training in meditation techniques, and the entire staff participates. This simple but effective wellness activity alleviates the high levels of stress among students and staff.

Visitacion Valley has received national recognition for implementing this transformative program, and the school points to the implementation of meditation as a turning point in its history.

Visitacion Valley's culture of affirmation and optimism fosters learning, embraces diversity, creates hope, and pays homage to the struggles of all students and their parents.

Preparation and Exploration

Reflection

Fearless leaders who are soul friends uncover the hidden potential of others. They shift perspective to believe in students' intellectual ability. They surface and affirm students' and teachers' strengths. They cultivate belonging. How do you think your school would transform if you could surface your students' and teachers' inner potential and ambitions? How would this surfacing make school a more affirming experience? Share your responses with the entire team.

Call to Action

Consider conducting one or more of the following actions with your leadership team.

Action 1. Soul friends and affirmations draw their positive energy from the same source: belief in the innate merit and worth of others. Create and distribute affirmations to one another. Create a protocol to help students write affirmations for themselves and their peers.

Action 2. Conduct a team strengths-and-values audit.

1. Ask each team member to self-identify five personal strengths and five personal values, writing each one on a separate index card or sticky note.

2. Collect, shuffle, and redistribute the cards.

3. In pairs or small teams, sort the strengths and values to determine commonalities.

4. Share.

5. Have each team complete the following: *We are strong in many ways. We are* _____. *Our values drive our actions. We value* _____. *We are strong.*

Action 3. Identify a schoolwide practice that negatively affects the school. Explore the beliefs that might be contributing to this practice. Then identify one or two strengths from the team strengths-and-values audit conducted in Action 2 that could be used to address this practice.

Action 4. As a team, discuss the following quotation from Carlos M. Azcoitia in the context of this chapter and consider how it pertains to your school: "We can't be cautious and extraordinary at the same time."

5

....

Fearless Leaders as Muses:
Inspiration in Action

When love and skill work together, expect a masterpiece.

—*John Ruskin*

Key Considerations for Fearless Leading

• What are the imposed conditions that define and affect urban learners?

• What do fearless leaders who reorient themselves as muses recognize and want?

• What does inspiration mean in the context of leadership and transformation?

• How do muses use inspiration to mitigate the negative influence of imposed conditions?

• What does inspiration in action look like?

• What steps can leadership teams take to reorient themselves as muses and to explore the landscape of inspiration?

Orientation: The Landscape of Urban Education

The Imposed Conditions of Students' Lives

Since the 1980s, urban school leaders have been able to depend on two things: scarce support and plentiful criticism. This toxic combination is not likely to be mitigated anytime soon.

In this chapter, we examine how policymakers and powerful anti–public education forces have hijacked the discussion about public education in recent years. In the wake of this ideological hailstorm, there have been significant changes in how the world views public education and how those in public education see themselves. These imposed conditions have poisoned school climate and inhibited academic achievement.

No Child Left Behind

From its inception, No Child Left Behind (NCLB) was driven by a constellation of flawed assumptions and misguided principles. NCLB is based on the premise that public schools are doing a shamefully inadequate job of educating students; that focusing on student weaknesses and highlighting the ways schools are failing certain groups of students in key subject areas will motivate students and teachers to improve; that public vilification and competition will inspire creative solutions to deep-rooted problems; that fear of reprisals and punitive sanctions will spur into action what the law assumes are scores of apathetic teachers and administrators; and that a relentless focus on questionable means of assessment will result in high-quality educational outcomes.

NCLB accomplished what it set out to do. Fueled by a deficit model of thinking, it uncovered deficits. Uncovering deficits provoked sanctions. Sanctions provoked fear (Jackson, 2011). No wonder little has improved. Falsely assuming that fear is a motivator perpetuates underperformance, furnishing plenty of reasons to be apprehensive, worried—even panicked—and stifling engagement, inspiration, and transformation.

Zero-Tolerance Policies

Growing out of the fervor of the U.S. government's "war on drugs," zero-tolerance policies are intentionally harsh and unforgiving. When applied to schools, they are misplaced and harmful.

Side Trip: Chicago, 2011

In the summer of 2011, a group of high school students from Chicago Public Schools decided to call attention to the excessive policing that the district had put into place in its schools. The students analyzed Chicago's school budget and determined that the school district allocated 14 times more money for security and police services than for college and career counseling, resulting in schools with eight security guards but only two counselors (Vevea, 2011). If budgets are a statement of an institution's value system, then what the students uncovered is testimony to a value system sadly askew.

School policies derived from the punitive mind-set of zero tolerance have resulted in increasingly close—and costly—relations between schools and law enforcement. This alliance has rendered public school students one of the most "policed" groups in the United States, second only to prison inmates (Advancement Project, 2010). Shockingly high spikes in all manner of exclusionary disciplinary procedures and school arrests, often for minor infractions, have dramatically increased the chances that students will leave the school system only to become part of the prison system (Advancement Project, 2010). The Advancement Project report makes clear what any student or educator who has lived under this kind of punitive regime knows: these measures detract from the sense of belonging that should be part of the school experience, and there is no evidence showing that they promote school safety or increase academic performance.

The Role of the Media

Leaders in urban schools must not only counteract the realities of their students' lives and the fallout of misguided policies but also battle against purposeful misrepresentation often fueled by self-interest: sell more newspapers, privatize public education.

Media assaults on public education are a national pastime. No one would deny that conditions in many urban schools are dire. What is under debate is how these schools are portrayed and who should be blamed for the problems. The media love stories of student violence and school failure, especially if they can blame these conditions on students, teachers, and administrators. Failing that, they will gladly blame incompetent parenting. They have swallowed wholesale what many private institutions, poised to make a killing in the developing industry of education-for-profit, portray as a dismal record of academic achievement in public schools fostered by an army of uncaring, incompetent, and lazy educators.

Private-Sector Interests

The private sector desperately wants a piece of the $500-billion-plus a year it costs to fund K–12 public education in the United States. A handful of private philanthropies have commandeered the national conversation around public education to include their goals: choice, competition, deregulation, high-stakes standardized testing, merit pay, firing teachers, and closing schools when test scores stagnate. When evidence is clear that their reforms do not work, they retreat from in-depth conversations about why and resort instead to a mantra-like repetition that U.S. schools are failing, that U.S. students are trailing behind their peers in other nations. The reality is significantly more nuanced and calls for a deeper, more wide-ranging search for solutions.

In her meta-analysis of two international studies on student achievement in reading, math, and science—Progress in International Reading Literacy Studies (2006) and Trends in International Math and Science Study (2006)—Joanne Barkan (2011) found that U.S. students in schools with a poverty rate below 10 percent ranked first in reading, first in science, and third in mathematics. Rankings dropped as poverty rates increased. The problem, it seems, is not public schools; it is the ignored effects of poverty. There is no will in the current political and economic climate to tackle the real culprit. Where profits are concerned, facts will be distorted.

Consistently ignoring or misidentifying the issues leads to wrong solutions. Both the media and private interests have successfully diverted the national conversation away from the real issue: how can the United States provide high-quality, meaningful learning experiences that enable all students to reach their potential?

Reorientation: Fearless Leaders as Muses Who Inspire

What Do Muses Recognize and Want?

Counteracting the combined detrimental effects of the realities of students' lives, the negative conditions imposed by policy, and the questionable motives of certain vested interests requires more than just the insight and affirmation of soul friends. It requires leaders who can restore dreams, who can add poetry to day-to-day endeavors, who can inspire aspiration, and who can fire up the imagination. It requires leaders who purposely reorient themselves as muses.

In Greek mythology, muses were the keepers of knowledge and the source of inspiration. The artist and the muse hold high expectations of each other. When the artist calls upon the muse, the expectation is that the muse will respond with something profound: a new perspective, a surprising twist. When the muse does respond, the expectation is that the artist will use the response to transform his or her art to a new and elevated level.

Leaders who are committed to reorienting themselves as muses are inspiring leaders. They understand that

• The realities and myths under which students and teachers live have a profound influence on the way students learn and teachers teach.

• Inspiration is impossible to see and impossible to miss. We have all experienced the transformative but elusive power of inspiration, and we have all suffered under the grueling tedium that characterizes life under leaders who lack inspiration.

• Transformation requires restoration of the spirit. *Spirare,* the Latin root for inspiration, means to breathe, an action necessary to sustain life. As its root word suggests, inspiration is about breathing new life into people and the institutions they serve. Inspiration is essential to reawaken those who have been systematically stripped of their confidence and their original attraction to high-minded beliefs by policies such as zero tolerance and NCLB and by the relentless misrepresentation by those who stand to gain from the defamation of public education.

Muses attempt to transcend the ordinary by

• Promoting the use of strengths. One of the primary tasks of leadership is to affirm strengths, but unless these strengths are put into motion, they will dwindle and diminish. Inspirational leaders possess a nagging sense that things could be better and are personally alert to possibilities. Sometimes this sense manifests itself as an intuitive understanding of what students and teachers need and crave, but muses are reluctant to craft solutions for others. Instead, they encourage others to use their strengths to accomplish both personal and institutional change.

• Bypassing reality. Muses are grounded in reality, but they do not let reality get in the way of their vision. Inspirational leaders are on a quest to find a solution to what others may view as outsize impediments, a solution that addresses needs that teachers and students may not even recognize and that directly addresses the often-debilitating context of your school and community. The muse sees the mountain of harsh realities as surmountable through creative and imaginative interventions.

• Renewing spirit. Muses are restlessly driven to awaken optimism, confidence, expectation, and anticipation in others.

As a muse, you inspire others. Your goal is to rekindle moral purpose, fan the fires of intellectual engagement, and restore hope, trust, love, and joy to two crucial, highly reciprocal activities: learning and teaching.

Things to See and Do: Transformation Through Inspiration

We believe that inspirational leadership can be a learned leadership stance: a cultivated set of dispositions and behaviors. One way to cultivate inspirational leadership is to tease out of the complex web of behaviors that constitute inspiration those unmistakable threads that weave in and out of the stories of inspirational leaders. Culling and analyzing these threads suggest behaviors that leaders who wish to inspire may adopt. We have found that inspirational leaders do follow a formula of sorts that guides their behavior and the behavior of those they lead. Put simply, inspirational leaders know the way, show the way, and get out of the way.

Side Trip: Minneapolis, 2006

Several years ago, in an after-hours hotel-room gathering in Minneapolis, a group of conference participants—committed urban educators from all over the country—had a chance to interact with a group of educational giants: Reuven Feuerstein, Art Costa, Sonia Nieto, and David Hyerle, to name a few. One participant asked Asa Hilliard—the brilliant, influential, and inspiring cognitive psychologist and Egyptologist—an earnest, heart-felt question: "What do we need to do to transform schools for students?" His reply was shocking in its simplicity and profound in its implications. He said, "We need to start by loving our students."

"Love?" you might ask. Where does *that* word appear in government policy tomes, state funding formulas, school board directives, or school handbooks and codes of conduct? In any event, what does love have to do with test scores, adequate yearly progress (AYP) goals, or report cards? The answer is, love has nothing to do with the test score/AYP/report card equation. But it has everything to do with community, learning, inspiration, and school-dependent students. An interesting by-product of love is that it emancipates and empowers both the object and the giver of love. It is transformative—and it is free. It can be cultivated by anyone with big dreams, big ears willing to listen, and a big heart willing to love.

This small vignette packs in many aspects of inspiration. The participant who asked Dr. Hilliard's advice is not unlike the artist stymied by lost creativity. She intentionally sought the advice of a muse, and Dr. Hilliard did not disappoint. His advice was surprising, yet it sounded sensible, and it required a completely different orientation. She had high expectations that Dr. Hilliard would have an answer, and Dr. Hilliard had high expectations that she and everyone else in the room would take his advice and figure out ways to insert love into the educational equation.

Dr. Hilliard's words were a catalyst to our developing a different under-standing of pedagogy. They expanded and intensified our notions of vision, mission, and commitment. They shut out other people's notions of who we are, what we do, and what we need to do. They provided the impetus to refocus our efforts and at the same time pried open a portal to new pos-sibilities. They enabled us to see differently, but they did not provide solu-tions. They inclined us toward a new direction, but they left how to get there up to our own creativity and problem-solving skills. In short, they inspired us. Dr. Hilliard, like all inspirational leaders, knew what we craved, and he fearlessly provided it.

Know the Way

The nine muses of old were considered specialists, each one an authority on a branch of the arts, history, or science. No single muse was considered the ultimate or sole authority on all of these realms. Each realm is complex and demanding, requires specialized training and ways of looking at the world, and adds a different dimension to life. Like the ancient muses, no individual school leader can possess the entire range of skills, knowledge, and dispositions necessary for inspirational leadership. The purposeful cultivation of leadership teams provides the possibility of leadership informed by specialists, whose combined knowledge is more powerful and transformative than what one person can achieve.

Understand human motivation, organizational behavior, and the change process. As a muse, you use human capital wisely—that is, you encourage those with different skills and propensities to become experts in different aspects of leadership. Someone on the team needs to be the muse of human motivation. Another needs to penetrate the mysteries of organizational behavior. Others must master the tangle of theories relating to the change process. When all these muses become immersed in their respective areas of expertise while being guided by the same overarching values, your team will be effective.

Understand learning and teaching. As a muse, you have a deep thirst to understand how learning occurs and what influences it, and a great desire to use this information to guide pedagogy in every classroom in your building. You also have an uncanny ability to ferret out and make clear the theories and practices that have the greatest effect on transforming ingrained definitions of learning and teaching and entrenched ways of doing things.

Build cohesiveness. The process of learning and teaching is an intricate stew, mixing attitudes, beliefs, and dispositions with physical, social, and emotional components. As a muse, you successfully present a cohesive theory of learning, a consistent and empowering belief system, support to develop practices that reflect the high operational practices of the Pedagogy of Confidence, and a clear set of well-articulated outcomes focused on high expectations.

Participate in professional learning as a co-learner. As a muse, you make professional learning a priority—the focus of your leadership team activities and the major work of all of the professionals in the building. When you play an active role in professional learning, you inspire others. Your presence demonstrates commitment, while learning alongside teachers shatters positional barriers, forges connections, and increases your credibility as a co-expert in instruction. By volunteering to teach a demonstration lesson, you show that taking a risk is something everyone can do. By employing strategies that reflect the high operational practices of the Pedagogy of Confidence as part of the day-to-day operation of the school, you demonstrate their importance. In short, you inspire teachers to commit to examining and improving their practice and pedagogy.

Show the Way

Inspirational leaders walk the walk. When your team thinks, acts, and speaks with one voice consistently focused on the positive, gashes appear in the cloak of cynicism that often envelops a school. By modeling desired thoughts and behaviors, you furnish the inspiration needed to motivate teachers and students to think and act in transformed ways.

Hold high expectations for self and others. As a muse, you draw your potency from soundly grounded beliefs, attitudes, and skills, which you use to stimulate, encourage, and motivate yourself and others.

Remain alert to possibilities. As an inspirational leader, you see potential in the bleakest situations. You search for solutions rather than bemoan unfortunate conditions. You use every available personal resource to uncover what is doable, fulfilling, and just plain right. You listen and look, read and reflect as part of an ongoing process to find a way that works for your community, your school, and your students. Remaining alert to possibilities creates a positive energy that is infectious.

Reshape the conversation. As an inspirational leader, you care about language. You carefully monitor the lexicon foisted upon your school and your students by others, you work diligently to eliminate terms designed to classify or marginalize, and you substitute words that paint a realistic picture of the situation or that have the power to inspire. Marginalizing terms include *minority students* instead of *students of color* (or the specific ethnicity, such as Latino or Latina); *low achiever* instead of *underachiever*; and *disadvantaged* instead of *school-dependent* (Jackson, 2011). Even the term *homework* can become marginalizing when one considers the number of students who do not have homes to go to at night or for whom home is not a safe place to do work of any sort, let alone schoolwork.

As a fearless leader, you purposely use language to inspire your students and teachers. In one urban school district we know, students are referred to as "scholars," a word that conjures up images of committed intellectuals purposefully and passionately pursuing the life of the mind. Along with using new terminology that eliminates marginalizing labels, you treat students and teachers in a manner consistent with the new terms. As Peter Johnston (2004) says, "The way we interact with children and arrange for them to interact shows them what kinds of people we think they are and gives them opportunities to practice being those kinds of people" (p. 79). If we treat them like scholars, they will behave like scholars.

Get Out of the Way

Students and teachers alike yearn for autonomy and self-efficacy. As a muse, you enable students and teachers to jettison the heavy baggage of dependency and replace it with self-determination. You use inspiration to set high expectations, making it clear that students and teachers will apply their strengths in meaningful, productive, and transformative ways. Then you get out of the way.

Provide latitude. As a muse, you yield the floor, encouraging students and teachers to broadcast to one another and the outside community their stories, strengths, abilities, and aspirations. Your school can use faculty meetings, newsletters, various electronic formats, and community events as venues to amplify students' and teachers' voices.

Fearless Leadership: Professional Learning at a Glance

One school fighting a mountain of negative press and a historically poor reputation in the community mounted a highly successful campaign to project the real story of the lives of its students and teachers. Making use of the Internet and a video camera, students and teachers posted two-minute bios in which they explained who they were, where they came from, and what their dreams were. The Two-Minute Bio campaign dramatically changed the way teachers and students saw themselves and one another and the way the community saw them.

Move, suggest, incline. Ask people to describe a major social, political, or religious movement, and they will undoubtedly talk about inspirational leaders who moved others to action. Ask educators to describe an inspirational educational leader, and they will generally recall someone who effected major change: the superintendent who computerized the school system in the early 1980s, the principal who ruptured professional isolation by introducing professional learning communities, or the principal who dramatically reduced school violence by bringing in grandmothers as security guards (Noguera, 2008). Inspiration, vision, and movement are intricately intertwined and essential for transformation.

Encourage cooperation. As a muse, you incline others to reach a common goal through cooperation. You put in place the organizational structures that spotlight cooperation as a shared value. The formation of your leadership team is one powerful way to deliver the message that the work of learning and leading is a shared responsibility. You do not reserve cooperation for items that are on the periphery of school business. You court the involvement of community members and students in the core business of schooling, an effort that takes courage, careful planning, and concerted effort.

Open up space. As an inspirational leader, you understand the four qualities Americans want from their leaders: trust, compassion, stability, and hope. You also appreciate that people are significantly more productive when they are assigned tasks that draw on their strengths (Rath & Conchie, 2009). Keeping these insights in mind, you create a new leadership landscape that provides accessible, open space for members of the school to draw on their sense of leadership and make use of their strengths.

Imagine a school where learning is joyful, deep, and fulfilling; where students and teachers throw themselves into the same intellectually demanding, authentic problems that make up the life work of experts; where students' thirst for knowledge and teachers' creativity guide curriculum. This inspired school supports self-directed learning and self-actualization. In this school, students and teachers are trusted, relationships are solid, and latitude is valued. This school bears the hallmarks of inspirational leaders who know the way, show the way, and, most important, get out of the way.

What makes these leaders inspiring is that they will take a chance on solutions that are out of step with prevailing beliefs but that resonate deeply with people hungry for a new way of doing things that aligns with their inner drives and prevailing values.

On the Road to Transformation

Inspiration Snapshot: Principal Marion Grady

Principal Marion Grady cannot drive any longer, nor can she read unaided the reams of paperwork that cross her desk or the mountains of e-mail that fill up her inbox every day. But if there is a professional learning activity taking place that involves her school, you can bet on three things: she will be the first to arrive; all teachers will be freed up to attend; and she will already have read whatever documents will be used during the session, having obtained them beforehand.

Without saying a word, she sends out an inspirational message: "If I can work around my impairment to be here, to prepare for you, and to be prepared myself, you can, too. Know that I set high expectations for myself, and, by extension, for all of us involved in this shared enterprise of learning and teaching."

Grady entered the world of education through the San Francisco neighborhood of Haight-Ashbury on April 1, 1960—and she is still at it. Although she has held many positions in school buildings and central offices both in the United States and abroad, her passion to work with challenged populations has remained constant. Note her choice of words here: a population that others might define as "challenging," and therefore a problem, she sees as beset by challenges handed to them, not created by them. Principal Grady uses her words as a reorientation tool that enables students and teachers to see beyond the obvious and uncover their hidden potential.

Well into her career, she had a choice. She could remain in the central office or return to a building. She chose the latter. Further, among the schools available, she chose the one that required the most effort. She knowingly and deliberately chose to be part of a social justice effort, with all its attendant difficulties, rather than retreat to a cushy office and be unavailable to offer students and teachers advice and support. Like most inspirational leaders, she understands the challenges her students, teachers, and school face, and she deeply desires to be in the mix, where she will be called on to provide the oft-needed nudge of inspiration.

The school she chose and where she continues to lead is a large building in the middle of a diverse residential area in San Francisco. When she arrived as principal, the school was outdated physically, and the pedagogy was stale. The building was dark and dirty, and each classroom had only four light bulbs and one electric outlet. Student performance was barely acceptable. As Principal Grady recalls, "There was not a lot going on here."

Today, the school's wide hallways and high-ceilinged classrooms are bright and airy and filled with student-created art and schoolwork. Teachers push themselves and their students to reach their potential. Teachers and the community have worked with Grady to create an innovative schedule that meets their students' needs. The altered physical environment and revised schedule are manifestations of the renewed spirit that permeates a school whose principal sees her role as that of a muse inspiring others to greatness.

Preparation and Exploration

Reflection

Inspiration comes in many sizes and shapes. Sometimes it is a spoken word or idea. Sometimes it is a thought that creeps unbidden into your head. Sometimes it is something you actively attempt to find. Think about a time when you were inspired to do something you never thought you could achieve. Consider the circumstances. Who or what was the inspiration? Why did you need inspiration at that time? What was the result of your inspiration? What do you think would have happened had you not responded to this inspiration? Share your responses with the entire team.

Call to Action

Consider conducting one or more of the following actions with your leadership team.

Action 1. Where do you see inspiration at play in your school? What are your students inspired by? What are your teachers inspired by? How might you build on these inspirations to transform the climate of your school or move toward your school's desired outcome?

Action 2. Inspirational leaders know the way, show the way, and get out of the way. Divide the team into three "expert groups." Each group will explore one of the categories of what muses do and evaluate where leadership in the school stands in relation to that action. Use the chart in Figure 5.1 to record responses. Share with the whole group.

Action 3. As a team, discuss the following quotation from Benjamin Disraeli in the context of this chapter and consider how it pertains to your school: "To believe in the heroic makes heroes."

Figure 5.1
Inspirational Leadership in Your School

What Muses Do	How Leaders Inspire	Evidence of Inspiration at Work in Your School
Know the Way	Understand human motivation, organizational behavior, and the change process	
	Understand learning and teaching	
	Build cohesiveness	
	Participate in professional learning as a co-learner	
Show the Way	Hold high expectations for self and others	
	Remain alert to possibilities	
	Reshape the conversation	
Get Out of the Way	Provide latitude	
	Move, suggest, incline	
	Encourage cooperation	
	Open up space	

6

Fearless Leaders as Ministers: Mediation in Action

Don't be afraid of opposition. Remember, a kite
rises against, not with, the wind.

—Hamilton Wright Mabie

Key Considerations for Fearless Leading

• What are the internal responses to the real and imposed conditions that define and affect urban learners?

• What do fearless leaders who reorient themselves as ministers recognize, and what are they able to do?

• What does mediation mean in the context of leadership and transformation?

• How do ministers use mediation to mitigate the negative influence of the internal responses to real and imposed conditions?

• What does mediation in action look like?

• What steps can leadership teams take to reorient themselves as ministers and to explore the landscape of mediation?

Orientation: The Landscape of Urban Education

The Internal Responses to Real and Imposed Conditions

In Chapters 4 and 5, we described two prominent features of the landscape of urban education: the mountain of harsh realities faced by urban students and their teachers, and the sea of ill-conceived policies, myths, and half-truths imposed on urban schools by outside forces. These realities and impositions have engraved a deep gorge in the terrain of urban education, marring the otherwise promising lives of urban students and their teachers. The poison of fear and the debilitating damage of distrust have paralyzed their spirits.

How do students and teachers respond? Shockingly high numbers of both bail out. Those who remain often do so halfheartedly or are filled with pent-up rage. The way policymakers frame the high dropout rate of urban students and the high attrition rate of their teachers affects how those policymakers—and thus schools—address this dire situation. As we have established, the language we use strongly influences the way we—and others—look at a situation. We have found that the term *exiled* completely reshapes existing paradigms.

Exiled Students

To be exiled means to be away from where you belong. Few people would argue that where students belong is in school, reaping the joy of self-discovery, uncovering the mysteries of the universe, and engaging in the pursuit of intellectual promise. Yet for many students, school is anything but a place of belonging. Even students who have not officially dropped out have often emotionally disengaged.

For them, education is a test of endurance. They do not feel affiliated to school; rather, school is a place to serve out a sentence of exile and boredom. The findings of an annual survey (Yazzie-Mintz, 2009) of schools all over the United States, rich and poor, urban and not, reflect this disengagement: the data reveal that one of five high school students has contemplated dropping out.

Pedro Noguera (2008) provides insight into the environmental and cultural factors that affect learning, not the least of which is the "gulf in experience" between students made to feel school-dependent and their middle-class educators. Little has changed since Michelle Fine wrote *Framing Dropouts* in 1991. Issues of race, gender, and class continue to be ignored in discussions of school affiliation and completion rates; students continue to be blamed for their lack of will to achieve, parents for their lack of will to support their children; system contributions to the appalling dropout rate are continually ignored. Indeed, in an address at the University of Toronto in 2009, Dr. Fine indicated that the adults who should care—policymakers, educators, committed community members—appear to be "anesthetized to outrage" over a system that excels in the production of dropouts—the most potent example of students exiled into hopelessness.

Exiled Teachers

Urban teachers are similarly exiled, deprived of the excitement, stimulation, and satisfaction that come from learning and teaching in an environment free of sanctions, constant monitoring, and a narrow sense of purpose. As an urban educator, you are intimately aware of teacher burnout and teacher turnover. You have undoubtedly experienced the ravages wrought by a system that fails to provide the emotional, psychological, and pedagogical supports that the caretakers of our most fragile resources—our school-dependent children—require.

The terms *burned-out teachers* and *high school dropouts* not so subtly suggest that teachers and students actively seek to leave a perfectly designed system. Further, the terms imply that students and teachers are responsible for failing to fit in, take advantage of opportunities, or persevere. Using the term *exiled,* on the other hand, leaves the door open to discuss the system's role in disenfranchising and pushing out students and teachers. One set of terms places blame on the individual. The second suggests that institutional conditions may be to blame.

Rather than blaming the victims, leaders who reorient themselves as ministers try to understand the victims' plight, decry the loss of human potential when the system fails even one student or teacher, and target resources to make the structural and environmental changes necessary to create engaging, welcoming, and supportive learning spaces. Ministers are eager to intervene—or mediate—to transform the environment and realize new, promising outcomes.

Reorientation: Fearless Leaders as Ministers Who Mediate

There are no shortcuts around the impediments urban schools face and their effect on students and teachers. We have already described two ways of circumventing these—affirmation and inspiration—and the leadership reorientations that support affirmation and inspiration: leaders as soul friends and leaders as muses. As important and powerful as they are, however, these interventions on their own will not propel a school into complete transformation. Mediation is necessary to accomplish this task, and leaders who see themselves as ministers are necessary to put mediation in place.

Mediation is a go-between that channels activities and behaviors toward a single outcome. Mediation is the overarching element that allows the process of transformation to occur, that connects the here and now with the distant and possible. Through mediation, leadership teams negotiate between the current reality and the future ideal.

What Do Ministers Recognize, and What Are They Able to Do?

The root of the word *administrator* is *minister*. To minister means to attend to others, to act as an intermediary. Leaders who are committed to reorienting themselves as ministers work on behalf of others in ways that enable others to work on their own behalf for continuous improvement, growth, and self-fulfillment. They understand that

• Turning around a school is not the same thing as transforming a school. Turn 360 degrees and you end up right where you started. Fearless leaders settle for nothing less than transforming their schools and the lives of the people in it. Transformation is about conversion to something completely different that is infused with a more powerful and effective energy. Transformation takes people to places they never believed they would experience.

• Students need intellectual and instructional investment, and teachers crave pedagogical confidence and prowess (Jackson, 2011).

• Attitudinal and structural changes provide the resources to ensure that students and teachers receive what they need and crave.

Ministers mediate by

• Interceding on behalf of students and teachers.

• Providing targeted, supportive, and intensive interventions to move from one state to another.

• Using the research on mediation to structure improvement efforts that touch individual students and teachers as well as the institution of the school itself.

Overview of Mediation

Our conception of mediation borrows extensively from the work of Israeli psychologist Reuven Feuerstein. Decades before neuroscience caught up with him, Professor Feuerstein posited that the brain is modifiable. He called this ability to change *structural cognitive modifiability* (Feuerstein, 1980; Feuerstein et al., 2010). Scientists now refer to this phenomenon as neuroplasticity. Simply put, new behaviors and actions deliberately imposed on the brain literally shape the hardware of the brain.

For educators, the notion that the brain is shaped by its constant collaboration with the world is a bold, hopeful, and positive understanding. For fearless leaders ready to intercede on behalf of students and teachers, the notion of modifiability is a concept to embrace. It has the capacity to affect whole-school transformation.

The revolutionary understanding that thoughts, experiences, and the learning process can alter brain structures has a downside, too. Our brains may be more resourceful than we ever thought, but they are also more vulnerable to negative and traumatic experiences as well as lack of enrichment (Doidge, 2007). As a minister, you mediate to ensure that positive modification takes place.

Things to See and Do: Transformation Through Mediation

As your leadership team reorients itself to minister to others, intentional acts of mediation become an integral part of daily interactions. Acts of mediation focus on a single outcome: the high intellectual performances that are catalysts for self-directed learning and self-actualization for all students (Jackson, 2011). Ministering to this outcome requires a complex array of competencies. First, you need to deeply understand the desired outcome. Second, you need to target mediation activities in three areas: the environment, student learning, and pedagogical practices.

Understand the Desired Outcome

By understanding the desired outcome, you will have a much better chance of reaching the desired state. In our work with schools, we have helped leaders become fearless proponents of a new way of looking at school for their persistently underachieving students.

Embrace the Pedagogy of Confidence. We have found that leadership teams foster profound school transformation when they focus their attention on a key outcome: high intellectual performances for all students. Along the way, they create mediative environments that cultivate the Pedagogy of Confidence (Jackson, 2011).

The Pedagogy of Confidence is the artful use of the science of learning to generate high operational practices that empower students and teachers to pursue high intellectual performances, leading to self-directed learning and self-actualization (Jackson, 2011). The Pedagogy of Confidence is a high-impact set of beliefs and corresponding practices that can radically transform—even revolutionize—student-teacher learning and teaching relationships, teaching focuses, and learning outcomes (Jackson, 2011).

Clarify connections. As a minister, you see the big picture and are able to communicate connections clearly. As a mediator, you will draw a straight line between the beliefs of the Pedagogy of Confidence and the nurturing values of affirmation, inspiration, and mediation and the outcomes they aim for. Figure 6.1 summarizes these connections.

Schools that practice the Pedagogy of Confidence see all students as curious individuals who delight in the exploration of ideas, creation of knowledge, and development of their beings. Teachers are viewed as professionally trained individuals, guided by humanitarian values, who have knowledge of neuroscience, continually increase their repertoire of skills that enable them to mediate learning for all students, and understand the relationship among culture, language, and cognition.

Figure 6.1
Connections Among Beliefs, Leadership Values, and Outcomes

Beliefs Underlying the Pedagogy of Confidence*	Leadership Values	Outcomes
Learning is influenced by the interaction of culture, language, and cognition.	Affirmation	By taking into account students' cultural and linguistic frames of references, we affirm who they are, where they came from, why they behave the way they do, and their culturally and linguistically shaped experiences, values, beliefs, goals, and attitudes. This affirmation enables students to be seen as whole and valued.
All students benefit from a focus on high intellectual performances.	Inspiration	When educators embrace this belief, their view of students changes. They see potential and possibility and dramatically alter their expectations. They push themselves and their students into more complex, engaging, and satisfying ways of learning and knowing. This belief is inspirational in the way it shatters delimiting myths and promotes possibilities.
Intelligence is modifiable.	Mediation	This belief is empowering. It holds out the possibility of change and enables teachers to be interventionists with the power to effect change. These interventions are the heart of mediation.

*Jackson, 2011

Mediate the Environment

Mitigating negative messages and experiences and cultivating trust are mediational interventions that alter the school environment. As a minister, you focus on creating the conditions that propel students to learn at high levels and teachers to elicit that learning.

Counteract negative messages and experiences. As a fearless leader, you know that your students initially arrive at school bright-eyed and eager. You also know that they carry with them backpacks bulging with debilitating obstacles and shattered bits of promise. Teachers, too, arrive at school fervently wishing to make a positive contribution to the lives of their students. Too often, the realities of life lived on the margins bleed across schools' thresholds, afflicting them with many of the same malaises that affect the community.

As a minister, you mediate on behalf of students and teachers by creating a bridge to learning and teaching—the bridge of a calming, reassuring, and understanding tone that permeates the school.

Create a culture of trust. Few of us are willing to embark on a journey if we do not trust those leading it. Before taking off on the road to transformation, fearless leaders seek to gain this trust. Trust is a catalyst for investment. When students and teachers experience trust, they engage with the school, with learning, and with one another. As a minister, your leadership team counteracts negative messages and experiences by providing affirmation, inspiration, and mediation to fuel belief, harness positive energy, build confidence, increase competence, and validate students and teachers as human beings.

Mediate Student Learning

The essential mission of schools revolves around learning and teaching, and the essential mission of mediators in school is to positively influence learning and teaching. As a minister, you mediate learning by ensuring that it is guided by the seven high operational practices of the Pedagogy of Confidence.

Focus on the seven high operational practices. In schools that practice the Pedagogy of Confidence, leadership teams work to faithfully and uniformly employ the seven high operational practices of the Pedagogy of Confidence. Implementing these practices helps ensure that all students will produce high intellectual performances. These practices affirm, inspire, and mediate.

The first three high operational practices of the Pedagogy of Confidence affirm students:

1. Identify and activate student strengths, abandoning the deficit model of looking at students.

2. Situate learning in the lives of students by acknowledging and making use of their culture, language, and interests.

3. Amplify student voice to ensure that students are heard, engaged, and affiliated.

The next two high operational practices inspire students:

4. Elicit high intellectual performances that engage the mind and animate learning.

5. Provide enrichment experiences that lift learning from the drudgery of routine and offer opportunities for cultivating interests, building on strengths, and discovering the novel.

The last two high operational practices mediate students by linking where they are to where they believe they could be:

6. Build relationships, the all-important ingredient that personalizes learning, cultivates trust, and enables risk taking.

7. Provide prerequisites, the supports along the way that strengthen underdeveloped skills, accelerate learning, and enable success (Jackson, 2011).

Mediate Pedagogical Practices

Teachers cannot single-handedly implement the beliefs and practices of the Pedagogy of Confidence schoolwide. As a fearless leader, you must put into place the mediational processes that will enable faithful implementation and integration of the high operational practices. We have found that cognitive coaching is perfectly suited to develop the type of mediation you will need to support teachers in practicing the Pedagogy of Confidence.

Facilitate development of the Pedagogy of Confidence through cognitive coaching. Art Costa and Robert Garmston's (1994) work on cognitive coaching applies Reuven Feuerstein's theories to teaching behaviors. This supervisory and peer coaching model is designed to capitalize on and enhance teachers' pedagogical processes to encourage reflection, goal setting, self-monitoring, and self-correcting. Because it draws on the same research base as the Pedagogy of Confidence, its foundational beliefs and practices align with what is expected in classrooms.

When you function as a mediator, regardless of your position (principal, teacher, or coach) or whether you are working with students, adult learners, or your entire school, you always follow the same processes. You

- Become alert to the current situation.
- Listen and probe.
- Avoid providing solutions.
- Pose empowering questions.

Empowering questions transmit an underlying belief in the problem-solving capacity of the person or group with whom you are working. You act as a mediator when you frame the questions in a way that expresses faith in the learner while subtly suggesting paths—not solutions—to get him or her to the next level of practice. Typical questions include

- What are some of your goals for this meeting?
- As you consider alternative paths for achieving the goals, which seems most promising?
- What personal learning or insights will you carry to future situations? (Costa, 2010)

Implied in each of these questions is the belief that the person being coached has goals, is capable of coming up with alternative paths to the goals, and has learned something or gained insight. Mediators intercede between the learner and his or her desired outcome by collecting data and providing feedback (e.g., naming the processes that good problem solvers employ) that enables the learner to gain insight and to self-correct.

Fearless Leadership: Professional Learning at a Glance

A leadership team interested in improving teacher implementation of the high operational practices of the Pedagogy of Confidence might structure a coaching session around the following questions:

- Which of the seven high operational practices will be the focus of your lesson today?
- What do you think would happen if you intentionally used additional high operational practices in this lesson?
- What might you need to research, or what steps might you need to take, to implement these additional high operational practices?

Cognitive coaching is a transferable process. Teachers who receive cognitive coaching can in turn use those methods in their instructional interactions with students. Cognitive coaching is, after all, a mediational tool. It leads to independent, self-propelled learning, whether a teacher is learning ways to enhance his or her pedagogy or a student is beginning the journey to think like a mathematician.

On the Road to Transformation: What Does Mediation Look Like?

Mediation is essential for transformation. It identifies a uniform and meritorious desired outcome, and it provides interventions and supports that enable students and teachers to reach their goals. It is not enough to name high intellectual performances as the goal and high operational practices as the way to achieve that goal. Teachers need specific mediation to their pedagogical practices to ensure that they are implementing the seven high operational practices effectively and with fidelity.

Mediating student participation in school is also crucial. We have found that schools that amplify student voice in meaningful ways optimize student engagement, which transforms the learning environment into an oasis for students (Jackson, 2011). In the next chapter, we discuss further how to amplify student voice.

Preparation and Exploration

Reflection

Mediation is a purposeful intervention that allows the learner to discover new ways of doing things. Think about a time someone mediated a learning experience for you. What was the context? Who was the mediator? How did he or she carry out the mediation? Share with a partner and then with the team. What new understandings do you have about mediation? What are the implications of these discoveries? Share your responses with the entire team.

Call to Action

Consider conducting one or more of the following actions with your leadership team.

Action 1. Revisit the section in this chapter on the Pedagogy of Confidence. Consider how the Pedagogy of Confidence mediates for instructional integrity and pedagogical promise.

Action 2. Individually, consider how your school currently addresses enhancement of pedagogical practices. Think of some schoolwide practices. How effective are these practices? What structures are in place to implement these practices, and who is responsible for designing the structures? Share your findings with a partner. After each of you shares, consider the following questions together: What role does mediation play in the practices you described? Compare the practices currently in place with the methods employed in cognitive coaching. What are some differences and similarities?

Action 3. As a team, discuss the following quotation from the Italian conductor Ricardo Muti in the context of this chapter and consider how it pertains to your school: "A conductor should guide rather than command."

7

Amplifying Student Voice

Our lives, hopes, and dreams depend on our ability to be heard.

—*James Bernard*

Key Considerations for Fearless Leading

- What orchestrated opportunities to be heard enable students and teachers to engage in meaningful and productive ways, and how are these opportunities mediational in nature?
- How do orchestrated opportunities for students to be heard relate to the goals of the Common Core State Standards (CCSS)?
- What steps can leadership teams take to orchestrate opportunities for students to be heard?

Mediation as an Antidote to the Status Quo

Every important journey contains not-to-be-missed side trips selected because of their breathtaking beauty, historical significance, or cultural merit.

Orchestrating opportunities for students to be heard is one act of mediation that deserves a separate side trip because of its novelty, complexity, and transformative potential. In this chapter, we explore how leaders can minister on behalf of students by providing them with the opportunity, skills, and means to have their voice amplified, and we explain how this effort can fuel the school transformation process.

Supporting "Radical Collegiality"

Mediation is a powerful antidote to the status quo. Fearless leaders who intentionally mediate students, teachers, and the school as a whole promote substantive and sustainable change, not by owning the process but by shepherding and supporting key players in their work toward transformation. According to Fielding (2004),

> Transformation requires a rupture of the ordinary and this demands as much of teachers as it does of students. Indeed, it requires a transformation of what it means to be a student; what it means to be a teacher. In effect, it requires the intermingling and interdependence of both. It requires an explicitly intended and joyfully felt mutuality, a "radical collegiality." (p. 296)

Transformation and radical collegiality require much of leaders, too. Leadership can stymie transformation efforts just as easily as it can promote them. When you mediate as a minister, you choose to be provocative. You become an agent of change, rupturing the ordinary to achieve the extraordinary. The leaders we know who have been courageous enough to put into place the structures and resources that amplify student voice have seen firsthand the way this transformative tool leads to radical collegiality between students and teachers.

Orchestrating Opportunities for Students to Be Heard

In typical classrooms, teachers dominate the discourse, exert full authority over what content the class will explore, and control the processes used to uncover the content. Eighty percent of classroom time is devoted to teacher talk, leaving only 20 percent for student talk—which largely consists of responses to teacher-generated topics, questions, and interests.

Such power dynamics shape experiences and relationships in schools (Dewey, 1933; Freire, 1970). It is our goal and the goal of fearless leaders to co-create spaces for change and social justice, particularly for those students who have been underserved and who have historically been labeled as underperforming.

For these students to reach high levels of intellectual performance and to become self-directed, self-actualized learners, schools need to make major changes in the way students are invested in the life of the school. For students to reap the benefits of intellectual stimulation and instructional integrity, they need to be engaged. For students to engage, they need agency. To encourage agency, leaders must amplify student voice and help students develop the skills to interact with adults in productive ways. We call this mediational process StudentVoicesNUA™.

The goals of StudentVoicesNUA are to orchestrate ways for students to be heard, to encourage students to go beyond their role as learners of content to become leaders of the community, and to provide opportunities for students and teachers to work together as co-learners and co-creators of the school environment.

StudentVoicesNUA is a centerpiece of the Pedagogy of Confidence, exemplifying the high operational practice of amplifying student voice. This particular practice merits special attention because, when integrated into a larger plan of professional learning, it has the power to radically transform the landscape of a school. The three facets of StudentVoicesNUA—shared professional development, enrichment opportunities, and student-led report card conferences—directly address issues stemming from the conditions faced by many students labeled as underperforming: alienation, low expectations, lack of opportunity, and lack of agency. In the process, they rupture the traditional hierarchy of school, address the brain's need to feel challenged and supported, and establish students as bona fide agents invested in their own learning (Jackson, 2011).

Shared professional development. StudentVoicesNUA takes a radical approach to professional learning communities by including students as co-learners with their teachers so that they can become co-teachers, a position that enables them to make the learning experience relevant and meaningful to them. Sessions address learning theory and lesson development based on neuroscience, the effects of culture and language on cognition, and the integration of these understandings into pedagogy that supports the seven high operational practices.

In follow-ups to the professional learning experiences, students lead lessons for peers and model lessons for nonparticipating teachers (Jackson, Johnson, & Askia, 2010; Sparks, 2010). Working with and as teachers benefits students enormously. They develop a heightened sense of self-confidence, gain perspective on what is happening in classrooms, and obtain insights into teachers' roles and responsibilities (Cook-Sather, 2007).

Enrichment opportunities. Providing students labeled as underperforming with challenging and engaging problems to solve and projects to participate in is the second facet of StudentVoicesNUA. These enrichment opportunities draw heavily on project-based learning, involving student-directed, collaborative investigations that make use of 21st century technology, include consultation with outside experts, and result in a product or performance.

In one such enrichment project, middle school students throughout the United States worked together to explore the myriad issues the world faces concerning clean water. Each student explored and became an expert on one facet of this issue, using the Internet and local resources for information. Students "met" their co-researchers via Skype, shared their findings, generated additional research questions, and planned products (such as a brochure about clean water and a series of school-based events to coincide with World Water Day activities) that would educate others about this issue. The catalyst of the project was San Francisco middle school students' explanation that they could not drink the water in their school due to contamination. Suddenly, this abstract issue became real.

Student-led report card conferences. Student-led report card conferences reestablish students as owners of their learning. In preparation for these conferences, students review, reflect on, and evaluate their performance. During the conference, they present samples of a range of their work with explanations about their performance. They share their learning goals and garner support from their families by developing a shared commitment plan to enable them to reach their goals (Jackson, 2011).

Although StudentVoicesNUA is a direct manifestation of the third high operational practice of the Pedagogy of Confidence (amplifying student voice), it puts into place all seven high operational practices. This rigorous mediational process

• Enables students to put their strengths into action (high operational practice 1).

• Encourages students to situate learning in their lives as they work with teachers on lesson design or deliver their own lessons (high operational practice 2).

• Elicits high intellectual performances by pushing students to reach beyond their normal performance level (high operational practice 4).

• Enriches experiences by giving students agency and ownership to open up new playing fields (high operational practice 5).

• Builds relationships among teachers and students as co-learners (high operational practice 6).

• Builds in prerequisites to ensure that students are able to engage in such complex, novel tasks as discussing learning strategies and explaining their performance during a conference (high operational practice 7).

Reflection of Common Core State Standards in StudentVoicesNUA

StudentVoicesNUA also provides an innovative way to address the Common Core State Standards in English language arts (ELA). The goal of the ELA Common Core State Standards is "to help ensure that all students are college and career ready in literacy no later than the end of high school." With this goal, the standards "lay out a vision of what it means to be a literate person in the twenty-first century" (National Governors Association Center for Best Practices, Council of Chief State School Officers, 2010).

If students are to demonstrate the expected outcomes laid out by the Common Core State Standards, they need to participate in activities that allow them to exercise these skills. StudentVoicesNUA provides these opportunities, as illustrated in Figure 7.1.

Introducing the Mediative Analysis Process

If the Pedagogy of Confidence constitutes a major desired state or destination that leadership teams strive to achieve, and StudentVoicesNUA highlights the important role that students should play in affecting the life of the school, how can schools unite these two elements and enable personal transformation for both students and staff?

One way is to include students and teachers in schoolwide assessment of instructional practices and school policies. The three-step process of knowing

Figure 7.1
Reflection of Common Core State Standards in StudentVoicesNUA

Common Core State Standards	StudentVoicesNUA
Students who are college and career ready in reading, writing, speaking, listening, and language . . .	How shared professional development, enrichment opportunities, and student-led report card conferences correlate to the targets of the standards
Demonstrate independence.	In student-led report card conferences, students select the work samples they wish to present and decide on their own learning goals. Initiating, executing, and controlling processes that were formerly out of their hands gives students a pronounced sense of agency.
Build strong content knowledge.	Because students are responsible for following up on shared professional development by delivering lessons in a variety of subjects and grade levels, they not only learn about pedagogy but also deepen their understanding of the content. As every beginning teacher knows, the best way to learn something is to teach it.
Respond to the varying demands of audience, task, purpose, and discipline.	Enrichment opportunities open up new venues for expression (video, radio, blogs, and wikis) and target real audiences (fellow students, teachers, and the community). Although the products vary, one purpose permeates StudentVoicesNUA projects: they provide a platform for students to investigate and express their insights, concerns, and perspectives on subjects that matter to them. During the clean water project, students took on many roles, from learner to expert. They faced multiple audiences, conducted different tasks for different purposes, and negotiated the language and conventions of the various disciplines in which they worked.
Comprehend as well as critique.	Shared professional development is built on a foundation of engagement and open-mindedness. Students engage in activities that give them a profound understanding of the content and the learning process, teach them to express their learning needs in a language that teachers will understand and hear, and spur them to challenge assumptions with sound reasoning.
Value evidence.	As the students who participated in the clean water project examined different aspects of the issue, they became experts on those aspects. They gathered and evaluated evidence, developed a point of view about what they researched, and presented their positions to their Skype colleagues.

(continued)

Figure 7.1 (continued)
Reflection of Common Core State Standards in StudentVoicesNUA

Common Core State Standards	StudentVoicesNUA
Use technology and digital media strategically and capably.	StudentVoicesNUA enrichment activities are awash in the use of technology and digital applications. These, in turn, reflect the six areas of proficiency identified by the International Society for Technology in Education/National Educational Technology Standards (ISTE/NETS), including • Creativity and innovation. • Communication and collaboration. • Research and information fluency. • Critical thinking, problem solving, and decision making. • Digital citizenship. • Technology operations and concepts.
Come to understand other perspectives and cultures.	One of the first reactions students have to shared professional development is empathy for teachers. Invariably, students will say, "I had no idea how hard it is to teach." This response is generally followed by self-reflection: "Now I will pay more attention in class." Teachers similarly see students in a different light as students provide insight into what makes learning work for them. This opportunity to shift their frames of reference is purposely orchestrated to bridge the divide between student culture and teacher culture.

the ultimate destination, assessing the current state of affairs, and activating a plan to help everyone reach the desired state represents the ultimate mediational act. However, for teachers and students to be competent and confident in this endeavor, their participation in the process needs to be mediated. Students need the language of learning and policy to be participants in assessing learning. Teachers need a clear understanding of why and how students can aid in school transformation. Both need practice and guidance in the specific protocols used to conduct these assessments.

NUA has developed a continuous improvement tool known as the Mediative Analysis Process (MAP) that provides schools with the practice and the protocols they need to conduct self-assessments designed to move them to the next level of practice. The function of the Mediative Analysis Process is not unlike that of a Global Positioning System (GPS). The beauty of a GPS is that once you enter your destination, the GPS finds your present position and continually tracks your progress. If you go off course, it adjusts with a gentle reminder that it is "recalculating." This recalculation, complete with a new set of directions, is mediation. Despite what knocked you off course, your GPS finds a way to reroute you so that you reach your destination.

Like a GPS, the Mediative Analysis Process is designed to get a school where it wants to go. It enables teams of interested parties—parents, teachers, students, and administrators—to examine student learning or any other aspect of school life to improve outcomes. It identifies where a school is and measures growth toward achieving a goal. The process, which is most powerful when implemented regularly, can be applied to individual classrooms, groups of classes (for example, grade levels or departments), or a whole school.

Here's how it works. Working in pairs or small groups, teams of educators and students determine the current level of pedagogical practice of a targeted area through focused classroom observations, data collection, and analysis. The teams use this information to determine the areas of professional learning most likely to propel teachers to the next level of practice and to exert a positive influence on student learning outcomes. The following snapshot illustrates this process in practice.

Transformation Snapshot: The Mediative Analysis Process in Minnesota, 2011

On an early spring day, just as the snow was finally melting, educators from four districts in the Minneapolis area met with students and teachers at a local middle school to conduct their first-ever Mediative Analysis Process.

The middle school is one of two in its school district. The district, which is part of a voluntary desegregation initiative in the greater Minneapolis area, serves several diverse communities and has been struggling to ensure that all students perform at high levels. NCLB has only confirmed what school leaders and community members already know: on "standardized" measures of performance, white students outperform students of color, students designated limited-English-proficient, students receiving special education services, and students who are eligible for free or reduced-price lunch.

All the visitors came from districts with similar profiles, and all were actively striving to improve their own schools' current state of affairs. Through professional learning and leadership activities, they had come to understand the importance of student engagement in connecting learning to teaching. On this day, they were about to embark on an examination of student engagement at their host middle school using a process that they would carry back to their own schools. The goal was not to assess the school as outside evaluators. Instead, NUA was modeling a process to show everyone how to collect and analyze data for reflection, insight, and transformational actions.

Between the visiting coaches and the school's staff, approximately 30 educators were present. Joining them were 24 students in grades 6–8 who had been selected to participate by their peers. The principal had designed this selection process to be as representative as possible, intentionally bypassing the established school government leaders and instituting a more inclusive process. During lunch one day, he invited students to meet in small groups with their friends. Each group was to select a representative who would be a student ambassador for his or her grade level. In this way, the principal was able to ensure that all students were represented, regardless of how well they performed in school, how they self-identified socially or ethnically, what demographic category they fell into, or any other defining factor.

Once assembled, the MAP participants at the middle school got to know one another, revisited their purpose, and reviewed procedures. During this session, the Mediative Analysis Process would focus on student engagement, an element that frequently emerges as an area of concern among educators. Related to this focus area is the high operational practice of amplifying student voice. To amplify student voice, schools first needed to examine the current level of student voice. We designed the initial process to look at how student voice manifests itself in one setting—the classroom—and built data collection around a simple question: what are students saying in the classroom?

To examine this question, the participants used a 90-minute block of time to prepare for and conduct classroom visits, analyze the data, and make recommendations for future professional development and prepare a presentation of the process to their colleagues. This process was followed by an invitation for the entire staff to question the data and consider next professional learning targets.

Participants formed teams of five, consisting of three educators and two students. During one school period, each team visited three classrooms for seven minutes each. Only one team was in a classroom at a time, but a classroom could receive visits from more than one team during the course of the visitation period. In all, the teams collected data from a wide swath of classrooms, a total of 33 across all grade levels within one school period. During the visits, team members observed what students were saying and recorded student comments on sticky notes. They then placed each sticky note under one of five categories of student response:

- "I don't know" or silence.
- One- or two-word responses.
- One-phrase or one-sentence responses.
- Multiple-sentence responses.
- Extended responses.

After having visited two classrooms and noting student responses that fell into the same two or three low-engagement response categories, one student ambassador murmured as she entered the third classroom, "Here we go again." Her assessment was not far off. Once the teams regrouped and tallied their responses, the results paralleled her casual observation. As in many schools, student responses predominantly fell into the lowest end of the response scale (see Figure 7.2).

The host middle school prides itself on fostering academic rigor. Its website proudly proclaims that it offers an Honors International Baccalaureate Middle Years Program as well as a Gateway to Technology Program. These data served as a wake-up call and led to a series of follow-up questions: if the majority of student responses fell into the first three columns even when academically rigorous classrooms were part of the mix, what does this say about what is happening

Figure 7.2
Tally of Types of Student Responses

"I don't know" or silence	One- or two-word responses	One-phrase or one-sentence responses	Multiple-sentence responses	Extended responses
8	293	461	37	2

in classrooms? Is it possible that teacher questioning techniques, pedagogy, or course content are contributing factors?

With these data fresh in everyone's minds, the MAP participants began the process of creating a lesson together. Due to time constraints, students were able to work with teachers only on the priming part of the lesson. They had a clear goal in mind, however: capture students' attention and keep them captivated throughout the lesson. Students offered cultural links and strategy ideas.

Involvement of students in a Mediative Analysis Process not only improves pedagogical practices but also provides a means of authorizing student voice. To do so requires those in power to provide legitimate and valued spaces in which students can speak, to retune their ears to hear student perspectives, and to redirect actions in response to what they hear. To make these changes means restructuring the mind, educational relationships, and the institution as a whole (Cook-Sather, 2002). StudentVoicesNUA provides a practical means for schools to step out of their current comfort zone and open the door to amplifying student voice.

Points of Interest: Data Collection and Analysis

There are several data collection and feedback models that aim to determine what is really happening in classrooms through classroom visits.

One such method is instructional walk-throughs. Unfortunately, many walk-throughs have been corrupted by heavy-handed, top-down approaches in which school outsiders—central-office personnel or other visiting teams—descend on a school with clipboards in hand, roam through hallways and classrooms, and deliver pronouncements of what they see going on. Many schools experience these walk-throughs as "drive-bys"—invasions in which outsiders unfamiliar with the school context arrive en masse to uncover all that is wrong with the school.

Instructional rounds address some of the problems associated with walk-throughs in several key ways. The instructional rounds protocol calls for the host principal to determine ahead of time a "problem of practice" the school is currently focused on, as well as to provide a context for the visit. The visiting team is well trained to respect confidentiality, to record what students and teachers are saying and doing, and to offer comments free of judgmental or evaluative language (City, Elmore, Fiarman, & Teitel, 2009). The comprehensiveness of this model, however, makes it cumbersome to employ on a regular basis. In addition, although the instructional rounds model suggests using internal networks for gathering information, the implementation often commences with outsiders, leaving many with the impression that outsiders are more expert about their school than insiders are. Finally, using the term "problem of practice" as the focus for classroom visits has negative connotations for educators who are working hard to do a good job. It is not an affirming or inspiring term.

Internal buy-in and a school-owned process eliminate much of the suspicion, skepticism, and ill will that often contaminate an assessment-feedback-recommendation process conducted by outsiders. We have found that one powerful transformational method is to encourage teachers and students to participate in this process as self-mediators. Educators feel affirmed when they are given the responsibility to self-evaluate, and they are inspired to reach the next level of practice. Being involved in planning how they will achieve that level is an example of self-mediation.

We have also found that the process needs to be thorough enough, simple enough, and short enough to be used frequently. The Mediative Analysis Process is easy to use, encourages self-mediation, and is built around the practices of the Pedagogy of Confidence, thereby ensuring consistency of vision, language, and philosophy.

Preparation and Exploration

Reflection

With another team member, define *amplifying student voice*. Where do you see your school reflected in terms of amplifying student voice? Share your responses with the entire team.

Call to Action

Consider conducting one or more of the following actions with your leadership team.

Action 1. Figure 7.3 provides a summary of the profile of students who meet the Common Core State Standards in reading, writing, speaking, listening, and language. Review the descriptors in the left column. In a small group, consider

Figure 7.3
Reflection of Common Core State Standards in the Mediative Analysis Process

Common Core State Standards	Mediative Analysis Process
Students who are college and career ready in reading, writing, speaking, listening, and language . . .	How MAP helps students exhibit these characteristics
Demonstrate independence.	
Build strong content knowledge.	
Respond to the varying demands of audience, task, purpose, and discipline.	
Comprehend as well as critique.	
Value evidence.	
Use technology and digital media strategically and capably.	
Come to understand other perspectives and cultures.	

the ways in which the Mediative Analysis Process helps students exhibit the targeted capacities and fill in responses in the right column.

Action 2. Read the following quotations in the context of this chapter, and select one that resonates with you. With a partner, share your quotation and why you picked it. Have your partner do the same. Switch partners and repeat the process two more times. Consider as a whole group: What important understandings have emerged through reading this chapter and considering the selected quotes?

- "When we are curious about a child's words and our responses to those words, the child feels respected. The child is respected." —Vivian Gussey Paley
- "It is not enough to simply listen to student voice. Educators have an ethical imperative to do something with students, and that is why meaningful student involvement is vital to school improvement." —Adam Fletcher
- "A school is inclusive if every student is able to identify and connect with the school's social environment, culture, and organizational life." —George Dei

Part 3

The Destination

Every school that embarks on a journey to become an oasis of success will discover two things. First, every oasis is different. Second, an oasis, like a school, is a living entity. As such, it is constantly changing, adapting, and evolving.

Yet all oases share some common elements. Let's look at it this way: travelers to the same physical location are often taken by the same features—the quality of the French Riviera's light, or the colossal size of Egypt's pyramids. But other experiences around these common highlights vary tremendously, depending on resources, interests, luck, and circumstances. Often, too, these experiences blossom into other enriching and influential experiences. A traveler's first taste of African art or Spanish cuisine can be a portal into a new pastime, a passport to previously unexplored territory, a point of departure into a particular way of experiencing the world.

Fearless leaders have a destination in mind. In urban schools, that destination is best defined as a Mediative Learning Community, a shared culture of positive relationships and cordial reciprocity between educators and learners focused on high intellectual performances for all students. However, this destination is not final, nor will all Mediative Learning Communities look the same. Every oasis shares common features, but each is unique, and each adapts as new conditions present themselves. To thrive demands constant adjustment.

In the final chapters of this book, we provide some glimpses into what a Mediative Learning Community looks like. Chapter 8 discusses the defining features of this oasis of success, and Chapter 9 revisits Beardsley School to show what a school on its way to becoming an oasis of success looks like.

8

. . . .

Mediative Learning Communities as Oases of Success

The signs of outstanding leadership appear primarily among the followers. Are the followers reaching their potential? Are they learning? Serving? Do they achieve the required results? Do they change with grace? Manage conflict?

—Max De Pree

Key Considerations for Fearless Leading

- What are the features of a Mediative Learning Community?
- How can a school become a Mediative Learning Community?
- What are the indications that a school is becoming a Mediative Learning Community?
- What are the roles students play in creating a Mediative Learning Community?

Signposts and New Frontiers

One of the first indications that a traveler has crossed a state or national line is the differences in signage. As one travels north on the East Coast into the Canadian province of Quebec, *exits* become *sorties* and *miles* become *kilometers*. References to Lake George and Saratoga disappear, and signs instead communicate the distances to Montréal and La Prairie. These signposts are visible manifestations that a traveler is entering a new frontier.

Signposts are essential orientation tools usually found at crossroads, those all-important junctures where we must decide which way to go. A signpost provides important information, such as the direction and distance to a nearby location. It can be regulatory in nature, such as a speed limit sign, or it can indicate the route that drivers are on or approaching. It can welcome travelers to a state or city. Whatever its specific purpose, a signpost serves as a clue, a beacon, or a guide.

Welcome to a Mediative Learning Community

Theorists posit that there are three intrinsic motivational determinants to behavior. These are the need to feel competent, the need to feel self-determining, and the need to feel interpersonally connected (UCLA School Mental Health Project, 2002). When these needs are not met, teachers and students burn out, rail against stifling authoritarian control, and distance themselves from one another and the institution. To counteract these negative effects, Mediative Learning Communities maximize feelings of competence, self-determination, and connectedness.

What are the signposts indicating that a school is a Mediative Learning Community? In a Mediative Learning Community, the focus is high intellectual performances for all students, and students are authentic members in the community who are talked *with* concerning matters of pedagogy, curriculum, and the life of the school—not talked *about*. A Mediative Learning Community reveals itself in the ways students and teachers interact, the manner in which their roles are defined and played out, and the nature of the activities that occupy them.

In a Mediative Learning Community, all participants—students, teachers, and principals—are free to share their voices to co-create a school community that values strengths, fosters self-directed learning, and realizes self-actualization (Jackson, 2011).

The Features of a Mediative Learning Community

As travelers cross the border into a Mediative Learning Community, they see a vastly different school terrain, dotted with the following signposts.

Mediation. A Mediative Learning Community is purposely designed around the beliefs, practices, and structures that constitute the Pedagogy of Confidence. Its focus is to maximize intellectual potential while meeting the needs of school-dependent students and their often-demoralized teachers (Jackson, 2011). The entire school community works in concert to give careful attention to what happens on a daily basis, how institutional structures operate, and what kinds of opportunities are available to mitigate the negative conditions students face both outside and inside school (Jackson, 2011). These practices, structures, and opportunities are measured against a simple, consistent yardstick: if they do not affirm, inspire, or mediate, they are abandoned.

Learning for high intellectual performances. A Mediative Learning Community places high intellectual performances at the center of the school's vision, values, and goals. All objectives, curriculum, and support are designed to link students' strengths and interests to the content in ways that engage and amplify their learning. Members of a Mediative Learning Community understand that the development of high intellectual performances requires understanding the ways culture, language, and cognition interact in the learning process. They recognize that the product of high intellectual performances is self-directed learning and self-actualization (Jackson, 2011).

Community. All schools are communities, and each community has a distinct culture shaped by the beliefs members hold about themselves, their beliefs of how others see them, and how they see themselves in relation to others (Jackson, 2011). Members of a Mediative Learning Community seek to rise above both self-imposed and culturally imposed limitations, and self-actualization is a shared and reciprocal quest.

How Does a School Become a Mediative Learning Community?

The Importance of Signposts

One of the major tasks of your leadership team in transforming your school into a Mediative Learning Community—your oasis of success—is to read the signposts that indicate where your school is currently situated. This task is often difficult because it involves looking at dynamic data: the visible manifestations of how your school is functioning and how well students are learning in response to this functioning.

The deeper a school falls into the abyss of underperformance, the higher the piles of data chronicling that failure become, often leaving teachers and administrators shell-shocked and data-shy. Who can blame them? Most of the data highlight shortcomings and seemingly intractable problems. Further alienation ensues when outside "experts" review the data, analyze the issues, and recommend solutions.

Transforming your school demands the courage to identify your own signposts that indicate not only the current terrain but also the reasons for the terrain's condition. This process calls for a different approach to the data. Fearless leaders recognize that *data points* are not the same as the *point of the data*. The point of the data is to provide a window into the reality of your school so that everyone—administrators, teachers, and students—can engage in a reflective self-improvement effort that elicits feedback and provokes action. By working on data in a purposeful, open, and persistent manner, data become insight, and insight fuels continuous improvement.

One of the most important data points routinely left unexplored is the essential question of how staff and students feel about their learning and teaching environment. The best way to elicit these data is simple, if potentially uncomfortable. You just need to ask, "Who is more qualified to inform your leadership team about what is happening in your school than the people most affected by and implicated in its day-to-day functioning—your students and staff?" The answer is no one.

The Process for Identifying Signposts

Before your leadership team can effectively uncover and employ data to identify crucial signposts and guide your school's transformation, it must establish a deliberate process for this task and understand the rationale behind each step. Here, we describe the five steps of identifying essential signposts.

1. Cultivate a desire to know what is happening. The essential mission of every school is the same: to support student learning and achievement through education. This mission is especially important when large numbers of students depend on the school for academic, emotional, and social support. Therefore, what students think and feel about their relationships with teachers and how they are taught must be front and center in any transformation model. Too often, improvement initiatives muffle or dismiss student voices. Teachers, too, often feel like invisible entities whose opinions and experiences don't matter. Leadership teams need a certain level of fearlessness to wade into what students and teachers think.

2. Ask lots of questions. Ask teachers and students about their strengths, their aspirations, and what affirms them. Ask about student-student, student-teacher, and teacher-student relationships. Ask teachers and students how they think they are perceived and why they think they are perceived that way. Find out about students' preferred ways of learning and spending time. Ask how students spend their time in classrooms. As a team, make classroom visits and then ask questions about what you observed. In other words, do everything you can to generate questions that will uncover the signposts that illuminate the core of the school. Your team can ask these questions in various venues, including classroom discussions, town hall meetings, and focus groups.

3. Use surveys. Surveys designed to elicit honest information from students and teachers are powerful divining tools. Like questioning, well-constructed surveys uncover and affirm student and teacher strengths and paint a picture of the learning environment.

4. Conduct inclusive analyses. Involve teachers and students in the process of analyzing results. Sit both groups down—individually at first, and then

together—and guide them through a survey analysis, discussion, and discovery process. Consider including families and community members, too. Create protocols with guidelines that facilitate the dialogue and analysis processes. We frequently employ Thinking Maps® to capture and organize data and to investigate frames of reference or perspectives. Thinking Maps, designed by David Hyerle (2004, 2009), are visual-verbal organizers that reflect the ways in which the brain organizes information. They are powerful tools for making thinking visible, for providing a way to analyze information collected from individuals and groups, and for negotiating ideas and networking meaning.

To ensure that every participant has an equal chance to express his or her ideas, we frequently use a multistep protocol for collecting information. The process begins with individual participants recording their ideas or sharing ideas with partners or small groups, and then moves on to whole-group sharing or analysis. We find that this protocol both encourages otherwise reticent participants to voice their opinions and generates a quantity and quality of ideas that far exceed other means of stimulating discussion.

5. Elicit and act on recommendations. The responses to your questions and surveys provide markers that uncover the heartbeat of the school. If the heartbeat of your school is weak, the members of your school must come to grips with it and strengthen it. From the discoveries your team makes, elicit recommendations for next steps. What practices can you put into place to address some of these issues?

This five-step discovery process engages teachers and students in an investigation and inquiry model that inspires deep reflection, honest exchanges, and mutual ownership of the school. The sessions are mediated to help students gain the skills in adult discourse they need to be heard by teachers and to be seen as full and invested members of the community, and to help teachers understand why students should be part of this process and how their involvement will transpire. Students and teachers feel affirmed not only when others are genuinely interested in what they think and feel but also when others take the time to listen to and analyze what they are saying. This process holds high expectations of everyone—for teachers and students to commit to this work and for leaders to put staff and student recommendations into practice. Participants are more invested in working toward the common good when they realize that their efforts will be acknowledged.

Students and teachers can provide a rich vein of data if care is taken to consider who will be included, how they will be included, and what they will be allowed to speak on. Fearless leaders aim to hear silenced voices, use open processes that support genuine exchanges, and give wide berth to the topics being discussed.

Leadership teams interested in surveys can find out more information about NUA student and teacher surveys on the NUA website (http://nuatc.org/aimhigh).

Reading the Signposts: What We Have Found

The five-step discovery process for identifying signposts helps a school discover where it stands and how far it needs to go to become an oasis of success. We use surveys to uncover the signposts in schools throughout the United States, whether they are large or small; rural, suburban, or urban; on the East Coast, in the Midwest, down South, or on the West Coast. In conjunction with the school's leadership team and professional development participants, we use this information to design a relevant and meaningful course of study that guides professional learning and equips schools to achieve their goals. Over time, we have noted a handful of surprising, informative, and consistent themes that emerge regardless of the location or size of the school. For example, in a composite study (National Urban Alliance for Effective Education, 2008) of just under 4,000 middle school students in the Northeast, the following major signposts emerged.

School success. Survey responses debunked certain pernicious myths about urban learners. An overwhelming majority of students reported that they recognize the value of school. They indicated that their families want them to be successful in school (98 percent); that they themselves want to do better in school (93 percent); and that being successful in school feels good (92 percent). On the flip side, only 15 percent of students actually reported that they do their best in school. This finding shows clearly that tapping into students' and families' desire for school success would be a fruitful endeavor. It is also a warning sign: schools need to give serious consideration as to why significant numbers of students report that they do *not* do their best in school, despite the fact that they and their families see the value of school. Why are students not doing their best? What could schools do to inspire students to do their best?

School relationships. The survey revealed troublesome information about the quality of relationships within schools. Fifty-four percent of students claimed that students in their schools do not respect teachers. Further investigation reveals that this lack of respect often springs from specific teacher behaviors, such as suppressing students' voice or disciplining students in demeaning, disrespectful ways. Because "mirror neurons" triggered in students drive them to mimic the behaviors they observe (Feuerstein et al., 2010; Medina, 2008), school climate changes dramatically when teachers consider the underlying messages that their behavior toward students sends.

Relationships are troublesome among students, too. Forty-three percent of students surveyed indicated that students in their schools do not respect one another. The survey results make clear that student-student and student-teacher relationship-building activities are essential to enhance feelings of belonging and to open the door to risk taking. If students are not comfortable with one another, or if they feel stung by teachers' disparaging remarks, they will be less inclined to take intellectual or creative risks. Schools can help build positive relationships through targeted school-grown interventions like amplifying student voice and giving students input into decisions about discipline methods.

Schoolwork. Thirty-seven percent of students surveyed indicated that they do not find schoolwork challenging, and 23 percent said that they do not believe they can use what they learn outside school. These data alert us to the need to question the nature of the work students are asked to do, as well as the nature of teacher expectations of students.

Research (Jensen, 2005) indicates that the brain seeks challenge and engagement and that learning prospers when learners feel personally connected to what is being studied. Leadership teams might well ask, "What are the tasks students are being asked to do? Where is the rigor? How can we make assignments more rigorous? How can we strengthen the connections between curriculum content and student interests? What concepts can we use to bridge this divide?" Asking such questions is an essential exercise for schools in the process of transformation.

Student preferences versus school activities. Two series of questions on the survey relate to activities: one designed to ferret out the types of activities students prefer, the other to find out what activities students are asked to do in school. We pose both series of questions to determine the correlation between actual instructional activities and activities that students believe engage their attention. The survey reveals that the activities students actually do in school tend to be their least preferred activities. For example, students indicate that completing worksheets, listening to teachers talk, and taking tests are the predominant instructional activities they are subjected to, while their two most preferred activities are using the Internet to find information and watching instructional videos. Students almost uniformly prefer group activities to solitary ones, creative activities to tests, and Internet research to lectures. They indicate a preference for whole-class discussions, small-group activities, and project work—in other words, engaging activities.

When staff and students look at these survey data, they are often initially shocked and troubled. Long programmed to believe that they have no agency—school personnel often complain of being tightly bound by state mandates, district directives, and program requirements—they also initially think that there's nothing they can do about the issues uncovered by the data.

On reflection and discussion, however, they begin to see possibilities for change. They realize that no one from the outside imposes school relationships on teachers and students. Similarly, they experience a sense of relief and renewal when they realize that schools have the power to adjust what students are asked to do in school and how teachers approach academic tasks. Most teachers are surprised by students' reported attitudes toward school success. In discussions, they frequently reach the conclusion that student interest in succeeding is a vital point of contact that they could mine and put to positive use.

In the end, this discovery process, painful as it might be in the beginning, affirms students and teachers by giving them opportunities to say what they have to say, to share their perceptions of school life—and to be heard. The process inspires them to work toward self-improvement around a shared goal. And it provides a safe, mediative environment in which they can grow new relationships in a revitalized culture of respect and trust.

Snapshot: Bridging Two Solitudes

One day, in a high school in a large district smack in the middle of the U.S. heartland, two groups of highly engaged individuals pored over student survey data. In one room, teachers and administrators from feeder elementary and middle schools sat with their high school colleagues and reviewed the high school students' survey responses. In the other room, high school students were similarly engaged in reviewing the data.

The adult participants were asked to read over the students' survey responses and "punctuate" their thoughts, a strategy that involves marking the text with punctuation marks to indicate different reactions: a plus sign to indicate agreement, a minus sign to indicate disagreement, an exclamation point to indicate surprise, and a question mark to indicate lack of clarity or a need for an explanation.

In small groups, they shared, discussed, and summarized their responses to the survey, and then each small group shared its responses with the larger group. At one point, a highly charged exchange took place. Several high school teachers objected to the way the students portrayed them. One cried out that he could not believe anything in the survey: after all, a significant number of students had indicated that one of their preferred pastimes was reading, and he could never get his kids to read anything. A middle school teacher wanted to know why the high school teacher would think students would lie. The high school teacher shot back that the students obviously wrote down what they thought the adults wanted to hear. The room burst into action: one side, mostly made up of high school teachers, vociferously agreeing with their colleague; the other side equally vociferously agreeing with the middle school teacher. Finally, one teacher said, "Why don't we just ask the students?"

"Ask the students" was exactly what they did. While the teachers and administrators had been meeting in the all-purpose room, a representative group of students was reviewing the survey in the library. Their assignment took the form of creating questions based on the results and then fanning out with video cameras to record student responses to their questions. After lunch and a hurried editing process, the students, with the help of an NUA facilitator, shared the interview videos with the teachers and administrators, who, in turn, responded with more questions.

Before long, we guided the students, teachers, and administrators in documenting and exchanging ideas in the fluid electronic environment of a wiki and working together in shared professional development and inquiry to build bridges of understanding, dismantle silos of power, and unearth the rich resources found in genuine partnership.

Carefully guiding student and teacher dialogue on issues that matter deeply to both groups is an essential first step in transforming a school into an oasis of success. It jump-starts the process of becoming a Mediative Learning Community.

Are We There Yet? Reading Your Signposts

One of the most important questions on any journey is "Are we there yet?" In the case of schools transforming into Mediative Learning Communities, getting "there" requires each of the chief players in a school—leaders, teachers, and students—to transform their behaviors and attitudes. Your leadership team can consult the signposts depicted in Figure 8.1 to determine how close your school is to becoming a Mediative Learning Community. To what extent do you, as a leadership team, see evidence of each of the traits described?

Interpreting the Signposts of Fearless Leading, Fearless Teaching, and Fearless Learning

Although we do not intend the table in Figure 8.1 to be hierarchical in nature, we purposely designed it to discuss leaders first, then teachers, and finally students. We did this for several reasons. Because leaders are best positioned to invigorate the transformation process, we first describe the signposts of fearless leadership. Fearless leaders are often the prime movers of school transformation, helping to initiate the process and then providing the ongoing support needed to sustain transformation.

Teachers have a stronger influence on students than any other group. This influence comes through in their daily interactions with students, in the way their beliefs play out, in their expectations, and in the supports they provide. Therefore, we describe the signposts of fearless teaching second. Staff members of a Mediative Learning Community share several common characteristics. Above all, they are positive outliers—that is, they display exceptional behaviors or practices that enable them to get better results than their neighbors do, using the exact same resources. They are fueled by optimism and strategically supported by fearless leaders.

Figure 8.1
The Signposts of Fearless Behaviors and Attitudes

Fearless Leaders . . .	Fearless Teachers . . .	Fearless Students . . .
• Carve out the avenues that encourage and support engagement in the life of the school. • Influence the ways students and teachers interact and deliberately prepare them for these interactions. • Guide and model for students how to question adult behaviors, articulate their desires and perceptions, and share their frames of reference.	• Create an emotionally and physically safe environment that supports students' cognitive and social development. • Believe in the intellectual capacity of their students. • Generate new norms, values, rituals, and practices that reflect and respect the cultures of students and teachers. • Acknowledge the structural cognitive modifiability of the brain and employ the high operational practices of the Pedagogy of Confidence to support intellectual, cognitive, and emotional development of students. • Cultivate a sense of belonging and esteem for self and students. • Shape and promote curriculum and opportunities that develop students' strengths, interests, passions, high intellectual performances, and drive for autonomy. (Jackson, 2011)	• Demonstrate high intellectual performances and self-directed learning. • Play a key role in a Mediative Learning Community. • Cocreate the Mediative Learning Community. • Participate authentically with voice and agency. • Plan lessons together with teachers. • Deliver lessons to fellow students. • Deliver or copresent professional development to teachers, family, and community members.

The combined effects of leadership and pedagogical behaviors strongly influence student outcomes, which is why we describe the signposts of student fearlessness last. Students in Mediative Learning Communities have a different role and a different level of engagement than do students in schools that are not Mediative Learning Communities. They are not simply the recipients of whatever beliefs, practices, and structures are put in place to create someone else's predetermined outcomes for them.

The relationships among these three sets of behaviors and attitudes are interrelated and reciprocal. Once a school has become a Mediative Learning Community, it becomes difficult to sort out starting and ending points, which specific behavior is responsible for which particular outcome, or which group has the most significant effect on the overall transformation process. As leaders ask more of their teachers, teachers ask more of their leaders and their students. As teachers ask more of their students, their students ask more of their teachers and their leaders. And so on.

Student Preparation for Participation in a Mediative Learning Community

Teachers need a degree of comfort in working with students in the newly carved-out territory of a Mediative Learning Community, where students have increased agency and input. *The Pedagogy of Confidence* (Jackson, 2011) describes steps to help students clearly and confidently articulate what is relevant and meaningful to them, participate as authentic members of the community, and provide input instead of being spoken about. Teachers can put in place four steps to student engagement that foster fearless collaboration.

Step 1: Student voice. The engagement process begins with amplifying and listening to student voice. We encourage orchestrating opportunities to elicit student perspectives, such as student surveys.

Step 2: Dialogue. After students have been empowered to share their perspectives, we recommend providing opportunities for students to converse with their teachers about issues that might have surfaced that would benefit from the perspectives of both teachers and students, such as cell phone use in school. Consider also encouraging discussion about non-school-related issues like community or world events, which are potent catalysts for dialogue. These dialogues acquaint teachers and students with one another's interests, insights, empathy, sense of justice, and motivation.

Step 3: Discourse. Specific protocols and formats in a variety of group forums with faculty can optimize students' competence in sharing their ideas and perspectives. These forums develop students' language and presentation skills and enable them to express their perspectives in a more academic, adult manner.

Step 4: Guided dialogical thinking. Teachers and students gain a better understanding of other perspectives when they look at a situation through the other's eyes. Guided dialogical thinking leads students and teachers in problem-solving, decision-making, and teamwork exercises that shift their frames of reference.

Through these orchestrated series of activities, students gain the skills to successfully interact with adults, adults discover the latent potential in students, and each group develops an appreciation for the other's perspective. Students also invest themselves more profoundly in the learning process itself, gaining deeper knowledge about engagement and learning how to learn. Because the principal work of schools is education, these orchestrated interactions at first tend to center on instructional matters. However, fearless leaders recognize that school is much more than what happens within the confines of the classroom. The way students are treated on the school bus, in the cafeteria, or in the hallway matters, too. Fearless leaders know that unexamined norms and unstated prejudices exert enormous influence on the lives of school inhabitants, so they open up avenues for student participation in the full gamut of school-related issues.

Points of Interest: The Ladder of Pupil Participation

Fearless leaders understand that without participation, there is little to no engagement. When they invite student and teacher participation in important school decisions, they increase the morale of both groups.

The Ladder of Pupil Participation (Figure 8.2) provides a self-assessment tool that, when used with various groups, could trigger deeper discussion about the level of student participation in your school (Flutter & Rudduck, 2004). Knowing the current level of pupil participation in your school is an important way to gauge student engagement, but it is only a first step. Not only is the degree of participation important, but so too are the questions relating to the purpose of student engagement, as well as the criteria, standards, and norms used to determine the quality of engagement (McMahon & Portelli, 2004). Have student engagement activities been designed to improve student learning outcomes, to

Figure 8.2
The Ladder of Pupil Participation

Level	Summary	Description
5	Pupils are fully active participants and researchers	Pupils and teachers jointly initiate inquiry; pupils play an active role in decision making; together with teachers, pupils plan action in light of the data and review the effects of the intervention.
4	Pupils are researchers	Pupils are involved in inquiry and have an active role in decision making; there is feedback to and discussion with pupils regarding the findings drawn from the data.
3	Pupils are active participants	Teachers initiate inquiry and interpret the data; pupils take some role in decision making; there is likely to be some feedback to pupils on the findings drawn from the data.
2	Pupils listened to	Pupils are a source of data; teachers respond to data, but pupils are not involved in discussion of findings; there may be no feedback to pupils; teachers act on the findings drawn from the data.
1	Pupils not consulted	Key decisions regarding policy and instructional practices reside solely with adults.

Source: From *Consulting Pupils: What's in It for Schools?*, by J. Flutter and J. Rudduck, 2004, London: Routledge. © 2004 by Julia Flutter and Jean Rudduck. Adapted with permission.

make the school look good, or to break down barriers to student empowerment? The first two purposes may slightly improve the status quo, but the third shatters the status quo and moves students into a position of constructing knowledge with their teachers, taking on controversial issues, and closely examining their own position in existing power relationships. Portelli and Vibert (2002) refer to these types of engagement as a "curriculum of life."

Preparation and Exploration

Reflection

Consider the ways in which being part of a Mediative Learning Community would support and accentuate your strengths, your colleagues' strengths, and your students' strengths. Share your responses with the entire team.

Call to Action

Consider conducting one or more of the following actions with your leadership team.

Action 1. Review the Ladder of Pupil Participation (Figure 8.2). Individually, determine the level of pupil participation you see in your school. Be prepared to provide evidence to support your position. Discuss your responses with your leadership team. What discoveries did your team make through this discussion? What are the implications of these discoveries? What could or should be your leadership team's next steps?

Action 2. Conduct and analyze a student and/or teacher survey in your school, using the NUA Student Survey, the NUA Teacher Survey, or any other reputable student/teacher survey instrument (for more information, go to www.nuatc.org/aimhigh). After conducting the survey, conduct inclusive analysis. Review the data using a protocol that invites honest sharing. Elicit recommendations and select at least one recommendation for implementation.

Action 3. Creating a Mediative Learning Community is a complicated process. Like most complicated processes, it involves many steps, inputs, and players, but the outcomes are worth it. In teams, consider what your school would have to do to create a Mediative Learning Community. Generate as many ideas as possible, and share your responses with the entire leadership team. Create a composite list that reflects the best thinking of the team. After sharing, plan the next three steps that your school will take to begin the journey of becoming a Mediative Learning Community.

9

Revisiting an Oasis of Success in the Making

> When you have completed 95 percent of your
> journey, you are only halfway there.
>
> —*Japanese Proverb*

Key Considerations for Fearless Leading

- What does a school in the process of becoming a Mediative Learning Community look like?
- What are the key elements of a landscape of success?

Returning to Beardsley

Fearless leadership is not easy. It takes great courage to exercise a kind of leadership that departs from the norm—especially in schools labeled as underperforming. Often, a siege mentality grips underperforming schools in a stranglehold that stifles creativity, experimentation, and innovation.

When your team becomes grounded in fearless leadership, rather than succumb to increasingly punitive and authoritarian measures aimed to turn your school around, you will turn to what you know students and teachers crave: affirmation, inspiration, and mediation.

Your team will recognize that a Mediative Learning Community does not spring out of thin air, that it must be cocreated by the people who inhabit and care about the school. No single set of prescribed steps results in leadership that makes a difference. Instead, fearless leaders and the schools they lead come in all shapes and sizes, possess unique contexts and challenges; and, most important, are brimming with distinct, often untapped, strengths. To be fearless in a landscape that is as variable as this one requires your leadership team to internalize a few key dispositions that will support you as you plunge into the heavy lifting of reculturing and rekindling your school. Key among these dispositions are the stances leaders adopt: architects, soul friends, muses, and ministers. Fearlessness will occur when your leadership team single-mindedly focuses on one target: high intellectual performances for students, teachers, and yourselves.

In Chapter 1, we introduced readers to the Beardsley School and principal Amy Marshall. In this chapter, we revisit Beardsley through a series of snapshots. These snapshots breathe life into the concepts of affirmation, inspiration, and mediation and suggest possibilities for your own work.

Beardsley is a small school. From the beginning, Amy Marshall made it clear that transforming the school had to be a joint effort. Because the school had had a long history of underperformance as spelled out in federal and state legislation, Beardsley was required to have a data team. Over time, the work of the data team extended to that of an overall leadership team. After all, the data were useless in isolation. They needed to be used in ways that went beyond the narrow interests of the legislation. Nothing prevented the team from using the data to uncover strengths or target professional learning activities, or from augmenting the data with information gleaned from the Mediative Analysis Process.

Given the school's small size, much of the discussion, planning, evaluation, and tinkering occurs during faculty meetings to guarantee that all faculty members have input. Since 2011, students have been invited into the process and into spaces previously reserved for adults.

Affirmation

Unassuming and shy of the spotlight, Amy Marshall possesses many of the predispositions that transform good leaders into great leaders. To begin with, she believes in her teachers and students, and she never tires of affirming their potential.

One of several affirmations that have become part of the life of the school is "Yes, we can." This mantra breaks through the mental boundaries teachers set for themselves and their students. At the same time, it affirms students who arrive at school brimming with enthusiasm and curiosity but whose life trajectories can be stunted and circumscribed by the beliefs of others. "Sí, se puede" is about shattering the crushing demarcations of others and intensifying affirmations that build on students' hopes and dreams.

Affirmation Snapshot: Asserting and Acting on Beliefs

When Beardsley teachers used to say that they could not expect much from their students, Principal Marshall reminded them of all of the Bridgeport students who went on to achieve great things, including the district's current superintendent, Dr. John Ramos. Her expectation is clear, focused, demanding, and uncompromising: high intellectual performances for all students. Repeated often enough over several years, this expectation has led teachers to look at their students differently. Rather than seeing their deficits, they see their strengths (Jackson, 2011). College banners hang in the bridge between the two sides of the building, a constant reminder that Beardsley students have the stuff to go to college. Successful graduates are invited to speak to students to affirm their own successes as well as the school's trust in its current students' future success.

Affirmation Snapshot: Taking a Leap of Faith

Fearless leaders are willing to take a leap of faith on the potential of their students, even when their initial reaction might be one of skepticism. In August 2010, we suggested that Beardsley students become colearners with their teachers during shared professional development sessions and then present lessons to their schoolmates. Principal Marshall's initial response was immediate and visceral: she reared backward, shook her head no, and said she was not ready for this. But after some discussion, reflection, and time to run the idea by her faculty, she got on board. Teachers and the principal selected six student ambassadors from among the school's 5th and 6th grade students. The ambassadors represented a range of ability levels but had one characteristic in common: they could all use a dose of self-esteem.

Beardsley's first foray into shared professional development occurred on Election Day 2010, when the student ambassadors came to school on their day off to participate in the planned teacher professional development activities. Since then, the ambassadors have taught classes, led professional training for groups of teachers, and assisted as presenters and facilitators during the visit from New York City educators (see Chapter 1), much to the delight of these visitors, who named student participation as a highlight of their visit. The student ambassadors even appeared on a segment of CNN's *Anderson Cooper 360°* (Perry, 2011), teaching neuroscience to teachers and fellow students.

Shared professional development provides an orchestrated opportunity for students to be heard, is a powerful affirmation tool, and is a crucial component of a Mediative Learning Community.

Affirmation Snapshot: Cultivating Ownership of Instruction

Beardsley's staff was not handpicked. In fact, by the time school enrollment was finally brought down to a manageable size, Amy Marshall had lost all the new teachers she had hired due to layoffs and staff reshuffling. Undaunted, she did what focused, fearless leaders do: she set out to uncover the pedagogical potential in the teachers who remained.

From the beginning of Amy Marshall's tenure at Beardsley, teachers felt that they had a stake in student outcomes. Since becoming principal, Marshall has focused resources on improving classroom instruction. Under her leadership, teachers have blossomed and grown. Faculty and grade-level meetings are devoted to affirming school progress. Teachers bring and discuss samples of teacher and student work that demonstrate their successes with new strategies. Once tightly shut, classroom doors are now open to visitors and colleagues as teachers proudly demonstrate their developing pedagogy.

Extraordinary teachers are being recognized for their achievements, including a 6th grade teacher who was named Teacher of the Year for the City of Bridgeport. In addition, she was selected as one of two recipients of the 2011 Theodore and Margaret Beard Excellence in Teaching Award, designed to recognize teachers who exemplify professional excellence, a commitment to teaching, and an ability to inspire learning among students, communities, and colleagues.

Teachers' involvement in various aspects of decision making, from data teams to professional learning, develops and attests to their professionalism.

Rather than leaving all professional development to district resource personnel or consultants, teachers conduct facultywide professional learning sessions. With their NUA consultant, Beardsley teachers learned how to structure and conduct a Coaching Carousel. Working in teams of three or four, each group meets with the NUA consultant and plans, practices, and presents the professional development carousel-style, which involves groups of teachers moving from station to station to learn a new strategy and explore its best uses. At the end of the session, the teachers engage in a grand discussion of the strategies' merits. Teachers decide on a period of time in which to try out the new strategies and then review their experiences at a grade-level meeting. The grade level then works on preparing a unified lesson that employs a set of steps we call priming, processing, and retaining for mastery: teachers use strategies that *prime* students for success, that enable them to deeply *process* new learning, and that lead them to demonstrate and extend their new learning as a means to *retain* what they learned. Everyone teaches the lesson and reviews how it went.

Another way Beardsley affirms teacher capacity to lead substantive change is to ask teachers to develop probing questions that help focus faculty meetings, professional learning activities and investigations, and the Mediative Analysis Process. One list of probing questions developed and researched by the faculty includes such questions as "How can we improve student achievement by increasing student engagement? What does active student engagement look like? How can we design and model lessons that build and sustain student engagement? How can we support deeper in-class collaboration among students? How can educators in a given grade level collaborate on a deeper level? How can educators collaborate on a deeper level across grade levels and subject areas?"

Affirmation Snapshot: Connecting Families to the School

The majority of Beardsley's families are Spanish-speaking immigrants. They feel welcome in a school where the principal, a former Spanish teacher, speaks their native tongue. In situations where language could become a barrier, Amy Marshall taps into her ready-made and easily available talent pool: her students. Parent nights and curriculum fairs involve students as docents, expert guides who explain and interpret the learning going on in the school. Graduates and families of Beardsley graduates are invited back to their elementary school to explain the college application process and to help families fill out applications and financial aid information, tasks that are overwhelming for families that have never experienced them.

Amy Marshall often says, "We have always believed at Beardsley School, 'Yes, we can. Sí, se puede'"—a statement that encapsulates her leadership values of affirmation and her leadership style of soul friend. Her simple motto taps into one of life's basic needs: to be recognized for one's merits.

Inspiration

Fearless leaders are inspirational leaders who take the stance of muse: encouraging, prodding, suggesting. Together, affirmation and inspiration enable inward affirmation and outward projection of possibilities.

Inspiration Snapshot: Modeling

In the spring of 2010, Eric, one of Beardsley's 6th graders, was diagnosed with a brain tumor. The entire school community wanted to raise funds for a family that did not have the means or the insurance to seek the medical help Eric required. Principal Marshall aimed high once again, establishing a fund-raising target that she knew would stretch the resources of her community. To inspire community members to go to extraordinary lengths to garner the resources Eric's family needed, Amy Marshall promised to go to extraordinary lengths herself: if they made the goal, she would shave her head. The community came through, and so did Marshall. When asked why she did this, her response was simple: "Eric could have been my child. Eric will have his head shaved. I will have mine. This is a small price to pay."

Although this is a dramatic example of inspiration, it is characteristic of fearless leaders, who inspire through modeling.

When Response to Intervention (RTI) was introduced into the district, principals were left scrambling to find personnel willing and able to provide the interventions and frequent monitoring of progress required. As a small school of 465 students in a district with a continually shrinking budget, Beardsley has seen its support staff dwindle over the years. Those who remain are on part-time schedules. How could Principal Marshall implement this program, which her students sorely needed, with fidelity? Her solution was simple. If volunteers were the only solution, she would be the first to volunteer. How, she reasoned, could people claim that they did not have time to volunteer when they knew that she has gone through four assistant principals in six years, that she is the nurse on days when the nurse is at other schools, and that she substitutes for her secretary when the secretary is out? Marshall not only volunteered for her turn at doing RTI but has also maintained a no-excuses policy for herself when it comes to fulfilling her responsibilities to her assigned students. In the end, Beardsley found all the volunteers it needed, and the students are reaping the benefits of this intervention.

Inspiration Snapshot: Creating Opportunities for Enrichment

In May 2010, after having listened to the radio broadcast that he and his classmates made during a weeklong enrichment project, Alex said, "When Ms. Alexis told us about this project, I thought it was stupid. Now I realize that I would have been stupid if I was not part of it."

The project, *Strong Voices; Strong Futures,* involved every 6th grader at Beardsley and resulted in a 30-minute radio show created, written, produced, recorded, and hosted by students that highlighted their school's strengths. As members of the production team, students scoured the school looking for news; conducted ad hoc interviews called *streeters*; made soundscapes; created "stings" (those all-important musical bridges between radio segments); wrote the opening and closing remarks; adapted *Where the Wild Things Are* into a bilingual, two-minute radio play; collected their musings in a series of radio diaries; conducted in-depth interviews with teachers about learning and teaching; conducted a heart-wrenching interview with a fellow student about how his experiences battling cancer brought out his strengths; and spontaneously created station logos just for the fun of it.

Each of these tasks required students to work under time constraints, but with creative freedom. Based on their self-identified strengths, they applied for and filled specific positions in the radio production team. They learned the demands and accepted formats of each type of presentation. They traveled the hallways armed with press passes, headsets, recording equipment, and notepads to document what they saw as the strengths of their school. One student, returning from an assignment with his team, shouted, "I feel like a CEO!" (McDermott, 2010).

Enrichment opportunities like this one enable students to display their creativity, individuality, and intelligence. Like all expressions of high intellectual performances, the results produce feelings of accomplishment and joy. Principal Amy Marshall and her teachers recognize the enormous power of enrichment to inspire students and unleash their potential.

Mediation

Fearless leaders who aim high not only affirm and inspire but also mediate. They have to. The gap between where they are and where they need to be is enormous. As a mediator, Amy Marshall provides the supportive and intensive intervention that buoys transformation and ministers to the needs of her students, her teachers, her school, and her community to get them to a place of competence and confidence. If leaders do not do this, who will?

Mediation Snapshot: Working Around Structural Obstacles

Fearless leaders recognize that achieving measurable and sustained success often gives them enough leeway to improvise and occasionally bend the rules to make things work. Once Amy Marshall determined her school's goal of high intellectual performances for all students, she moved into action, using the resources available to her. The district had recently partnered with the National Urban Alliance for Effective Education, an organization that would provide professional learning in line with her beliefs. The major means of this professional learning is site visits, where groups of teachers work with an NUA consultant in a process that involves new learning, classroom implementation of that new learning in the form of demonstration lessons, peer coaching, and debriefing. Site visits require time, and classrooms require coverage during that time. While other principals might run to the district office begging for substitute teachers they cannot have, Principal Marshall used whatever resources were available for class coverage. The school community's commitment to the cause inspired everyone to be creative and work together to support change when necessary. Teachers also knew that Marshall would work above and beyond to support teacher efforts and assist them when necessary, a sacrifice that most fearless leaders are willing to make.

Mediation Snapshot: Cultivating Competence and Confidence

Fearless leaders not only make their expectations known but also make the necessary school arrangements to support implementation. Once the structures were in place that paved the way for professional learning at Beardsley, further fearless mediation was needed. Teachers needed to implement new pedagogical practices with fidelity, which could happen only if they practiced them, shared their successes, and worked out the challenges. Amy Marshall made clear that she expected to see the instructional strategies shared by NUA mentors in lessons, on the walls, in the halls, and in the mouths of students. She employed similar strategies during faculty and parent meetings, devoting them to instructional matters and inviting parents to information sessions.

Mediation Snapshot: Moving to the Next Level of Practice

From the beginning of Beardsley's partnership with NUA, teachers have been involved in the Mediative Analysis Process. Rather than assuming that they are making progress toward more intellectually rich and challenging classrooms, Beardsley teachers look for evidence of this progress, which they then celebrate and analyze to determine how they can move to the next level of practice. This series of steps defines mediation.

To help teachers move to the next level of practice, Amy Marshall guides them in seeing connections between initiatives. As in most schools under scrutiny to improve, Beardsley has a data team. Research indicates that data teams spend much of their time uncovering problems, which they do very proficiently. What they do not do well is use the data to solve problems. When the Beardsley data team's deliberations uncover a problem, Marshall asks team members to consider what instructional interventions might address the issue. The data team accordingly plans and implements professional learning, and all the teachers examine progress. Fearless leaders look for ways to continually move the agenda along in supportive ways while helping everyone see the cohesiveness in the efforts under way.

Mediation is rooted in the belief that organisms and institutions can and will change with appropriate supports and clarity of vision. When the inevitable pushback rears up and someone suggests something that counters this forward movement, Amy Marshall says, without fanfare or rancor, "This is the way we do things at Beardsley." And this is the way they will continue to do things at Beardsley, knowing that success is not a destination but a spirit that drives decisions, attitudes, and outcomes.

Amy Marshall demonstrates all the key leadership stances that support transformation: she is the prime architect of Beardsley's transformation, and she is soul friend, muse, and minister. Her staff members make most decisions collegially, and she calls on them to affirm, inspire, and mediate one another, supported by her uncompromising fearlessness and unwavering belief in them.

The Landscape of Success

> Success is not a place at which one arrives but rather the
> spirit with which one undertakes the journey.
>
> —*Alex Noble*

As the quotation above indicates, success is not a place or an end. Rather, success is an ongoing journey guided by a spirit, a disposition, and a sense of values. Creating an oasis of success that enables school-dependent students and their teachers to thrive is a spirit-driven, continual enterprise that requires more than technical leadership skills, cannot be measured by standardized tests, and can profoundly transform lives. To nurture takes commitment—the kind of commitment required of a calling. Fearless leaders do not see themselves as fulfilling the requirements of a job. Instead, they see themselves as dedicated to a cause or a vocation.

Schools are communities, and what fuels them is a matter of choice. Urban schools have particular mores that leaders must address to transform them from places of oppression to flourishing communities of potential and growth.

Those of us who have the privilege to walk in and out of schools all over the United States know immediately when we enter an oasis of success. We sense its spirit. We react to the pulse of its positive energy. We sense the bonds of trusting, respectful relationships. Were we to look, we could easily spot the deliberate, genuine use of affirmations. We could ferret out the multiple sources of inspiration that guide and motivate students and staff. We could point to particular actions, stances, and structures that provide mediation.

The ambience of success is palpable, even if it is not measurable. Like oases thriving in otherwise parched and barren landscapes, successful urban schools stand out in sharp contrast to expectations and norms of what urban schools look like. When you cast your eye over this revitalized landscape, you will observe a purposeful design that affirms, a clear vision that inspires, and a deliberate plan that mediates. An oasis of success is not a haphazard occurrence; it is sustained by essential attitudinal, institutional, and organizational elements.

Continue to look, and you will see students and teachers who are content and confident, whose work together is marked by shared commitment and joyful curiosity. You will see schools that place equal value on the life of the mind and the nurturing of the soul, where the cares, challenges, and hurts inflicted by the outside world are held in abeyance.

Now is your time to lead fearlessly. Look at yourself as an architect able to envision, fashion, and nurture a transformed environment in which your students and staff flourish. Cognizant of the tasks before you, you can marshal crucial resources, one of the most important being your team of leaders. As architects, soul friends, muses, and ministers, you single-mindedly focus on AIMing for success: affirming, inspiring, and mediating the intellectual potential, competence, and confidence of your students.

References

Advancement Project. (2010, March). *Test, punish, and push out: How "zero tolerance" and high-stakes testing funnel youth into the school-to-prison pipeline.* Washington, DC: Author. Available: http://www.advancementproject.org/digital-library/publications/test-punish-and-push-out-how-zero-tolerance-and-high-stakes-testing-fu

Barkan, J. (2011, Winter). Got dough? How billionaires rule our schools. *Dissent Magazine.* Available: http://dissentmagazine.org/article/?article=3781

Barth, R. S. (2006). Improving relationships within the schoolhouse. *Educational Leadership, 63*(6), 8–13.

Bradley, R. H., Whiteside-Mansell, L., Mundfrom, D. J., Casey, P. H., Kelleher, K. J., & Pope, S. K. (1994). Early indications of resilience and their relation to experiences in the home environments of low birthweight, premature children living in poverty. *Child Development, 65*(2), 346–360.

City, E. A., Elmore, R. F., Fiarman, S. E., & Teitel, L. (2009). *Instructional rounds in education: A network approach to improving teaching and learning.* Cambridge, MA: Harvard Education Press.

Cohen, G. L., Garcia, J., Apfel, N., & Master, A. (2006). Reducing the racial achievement gap: A social-psychological intervention. *Science, 313,* 1307–1310.

Cook-Sather, A. (2002). Authorizing students' perspectives: Toward trust, dialogue, and change in education. *Educational Researcher, 31*(4), 3–14.

Cook-Sather, A. (2007). What would happen if we treated students as those with opinions that matter? The benefits to principals and teachers of supporting youth engagement in school. *NASSP, 91*(4), 343–362.

Cooper, E. J. (2004). The pursuit of equity and excellence in educational opportunity. In D. Lapp, C. C. Block, E. J. Cooper, J. Flood, N. Roser, & J. V. Tinajero (Eds.), *Teaching all the children: Strategies for developing literacy in an urban setting* (pp. 12–30). New York: Guilford Press.

Cooper, E. J. (2005). It begins with belief: Social demography is not destiny. *Voices from the Middle, 13*(1), 25–33.

Cooper, E. J. (2009). Realities and responsibilities in the education village. In L. C. Tillman (Ed.), *The Sage handbook on African American education* (pp. 435–450). Los Angeles: Sage.

Cooper, E., & Jackson Y. (2011). The fierce urgency of now: It is time to close the gap. *Education Week, 30*(18), 22.

Costa, A. (2010). *Mindful mediators: Conducting conversations intended to enhance self-directedness.* Presentation at NUA Summer Academy, San Francisco, California.

Costa, A., & Garmston, R. (1994). *Cognitive coaching: A foundation for renaissance schools.* Norwood, MA: Christopher-Gordon.

Creswell, J. D., Welch, W. T., Taylor, S. E., Sherman, D. K., Gruenewald, T., & Mann, T. (2005). Affirmation of personal values buffers neuroendocrine and psychological stress responses. *Psychological Science, 16*(11), 846–851.

Dewey, J. (1933). *How we think.* New York: D. C. Heath and Co.

DeWitt, P., & Moccia, J. (2011). Surviving a school closing. *Educational Leadership, 68*(8), 54–57.

Doidge, N. (2007). *The brain that changes itself.* New York: Penguin Books.

Dweck, C. (2000). *Self theories: Their role in motivation, personality, and development.* New York: Psychology Press.

Epstein, J. (1995). School/family/community partnerships: Caring for the children we share. *Phi Delta Kappan, 76*(9), 701–712.

Feuerstein, R. (1979). Cognitive modifiability in retarded adolescents: Effects of instrumental enrichment. *American Journal of Mental Deficiency, 83*(6), 88–96.

Feuerstein, R. (1980). *Instrumental enrichment: An intervention program for cognitive modifiability.* Baltimore: University Park Press.

Feuerstein, R., Feuerstein, R. S., & Falik, L. H. (2010). *Beyond smarter: Mediated learning and the brain's capacity for change.* New York: Teachers College Press.

Feuerverger, G. (2007). *Teaching, learning and other miracles.* Rotterdam, Netherlands: Sense Publishers.

Fielding, M. (2004). Transformative approaches to student voice: Theoretical underpinnings, recalcitrant realities. *British Educational Research Journal, 30*(2), 295–311.

Fine, M. (1991). *Framing dropouts: Notes on the politics of an urban high school.* Albany, NY: SUNY Press.

Fine, M. (2009, March 25). *When objects become subjects: A 25-year journey from laboratory experimentation to participatory action research with youth.* Presentation at the first annual William Waters symposium on urban education, University of Toronto Institute for Studies in Education, Ontario, Canada.

Flutter, J., & Rudduck, J. (2004). *Consulting pupils: What's in it for schools?* London: Routledge.

Freire, P. (1970). *The pedagogy of the oppressed.* New York: Herder and Herder.

Fullan, M. (1998). Breaking the bonds of dependency. *Educational Leadership, 55*(7), 6–10.

Fullan, M., & Levin, B. (2009). The fundamentals of whole system reform: A case study from Canada. *Education Week, 28*(35), 30–31.

Garmston, R. J., & Wellman, B. M. (2009). *The adaptive school: A sourcebook for developing collaborative groups.* Norwood, MA: Christopher-Gordon.

Hambrick, D., & Brandon, G. (1988). Executive values. In D. Hambrick (Ed.), *The executive effect: Concepts and methods for studying top managers.* Greenwich, CT: JAI Press.

Henderson, A. T., Carson, J., Avallone, P., & Whipple, M. (2011). Making the most of school-family compacts. *Educational Leadership, 68*(8), 48–53.

Hyerle, D. (2004). *Student successes with thinking maps.* Thousand Oaks, CA: Corwin Press.

Hyerle, D. (2009). *Visual tools for transforming information into knowledge.* Thousand Oaks, CA: Corwin Press.

Jackson, Y. (2011). *The pedagogy of confidence: Inspiring high intellectual performances in urban schools.* New York: Teachers College Press.

Jackson, Y., Johnson, T. G., & Askia, A. (2010, September). Kids teaching kids. *Educational Leadership, 68*(1), 60–63.

Jackson, Y., & McDermott, V. (2009). Fearless leading. *Educational Leadership, 67*(2), 34–39.

Jensen, E. (2005). *Teaching with the brain in mind.* Alexandria, VA: ASCD.

Jensen, E. (2009). *Teaching with poverty in mind: What being poor does to kids' brains and what schools can do about it.* Alexandria, VA: ASCD.

Johnston, P. (2004). *Choice words: How our language affects children's learning.* Portland, ME: Stenhouse.

King, M. L. (1963, August 28). "I have a dream." Public address at the March on Washington for Jobs and Freedom, Washington, DC.

Lackoff, G., & Johnson, M. (2003). *Metaphors we live by.* Chicago: University of Chicago Press.

Leithwood, K., Day, C., Sammons, P., Harris, A., & Hopkins, D. (2006). *Successful school leadership: What it is and how it influences pupil learning.* Research Report No. 800. Nottingham, UK: National College for School Leadership, University of Nottingham.

Louis, K. S., Leithwood, K., Wahlstrom, K. L., & Anderson, S. E. (2010). *Learning from leadership: Investigating the links to improved student learning.* St. Paul, MN, and Toronto, Ontario: Center for Applied Research and Educational Improvement/University of Minnesota and Ontario Institute for Studies in Education/University of Toronto.

Margolin, G., & Gordis, E. B. (2000, February). The effects of family and community violence on children. *Annual Review of Psychology, 51*(1), 445–479.

McDermott, V. (2010). Student radio: Magnifying voices, preparing a future. *ASCD Express, 5*(22).

McDonald, J. P., Mohr, N., Dichter, A., & McDonald, E. C. (2007). *The power of protocols: An educator's guide to better practice* (2nd ed.). New York: Teachers College Press.

McMahon, B., & Portelli, J. P. (2004). Engagement for what? Beyond popular discourses of student engagement. *Leadership and Policy in Schools, 3*(1), 59–76.

Medina, J. (2008). *Brain rules: 12 principles for surviving and thriving at work, home, and school.* Seattle, WA: Pear Press.

MetLife. (2011). *The MetLife survey of the American teacher: Expectations and experiences. A survey of teachers, principals and leaders of college education programs.* (ERIC Report No. ED496558). New York: Author.

National Governors Association Center for Best Practices (NGA Center for Best Practices), Council of Chief State School Officers (CCSSO). (2010). *Common Core State Standards.* Washington, DC: Author.

National Urban Alliance for Effective Education. (2008). Unpublished study. Syosset, NY: Author.

National Urban Alliance for Effective Education & the Newark Public Schools. (2011). *The justice epistles.* Syosset, NY: Author.

Nieto, S. (1996). *Affirming diversity.* White Plains, NY: Longman.

Noguera, P. (2008). *The trouble with black boys . . . and other reflections on race, equity, and the future of public education.* San Francisco: Jossey-Bass.

O'Donohue, J. (1997). *Anam cara: A book of Celtic wisdom.* New York: Harper Collins.

Perry, S. (Producer). (2011, May 23). When students become teachers. *Anderson Cooper 360°.* Atlanta: CNN.

Portelli, J., & Vibert, A. (2002). A curriculum of life. *Education Canada, 42*(2), 36–39.

Rath, T., & Conchie, B. (2009). *Strengths-based leadership: Great leaders, teams and why people follow.* New York: Gallup Press.

Rist, R. C. (2000). HER classic: Student social class and teacher expectations: The self-fulfilling prophesy in ghetto education. *Harvard Education Review, 70*(3), 257–301.

Roxburgh, A. J. (2010). *Missional map-making: Skills for leading in times of transition.* San Francisco: Jossey-Bass.

Sanders, W. L., & Rivers, J. C. (1996). *Cumulative and residual effects of teaching on future student academic achievement.* Knoxville, TN: University of Tennessee Value-Added Research and Assessment Center.

Solomon, D. L., Battistich, V., & Hom, A. (1996). Teacher beliefs and practices serving communities that differ in socioeconomic level. *Journal of Experimental Education, 64*(4), 327–347.

Sontag, S. (2003). *Regarding the pain of others.* New York: Farrar, Strauss and Giroux.

Sparks, S. D. (2010, October 13). Raising expectations is aim of new effort. *Education Week, 30*(7), pp. 1, 16–17.

Steele, C. (1988). The psychology of self-affirmation: Sustaining the integrity of self. In L. Berkowitz (Ed.), *Advances in experimental psychology, 21* (pp. 261–302). San Diego, CA: New Academic Press.

Steele, C. (2010). *Whistling Vivaldi and other clues to how stereotypes affect us.* New York: W. W. Norton & Company.

UCLA School Mental Health Project. (2002, Spring). School staff burnout. *Addressing Barriers to Learning, 7*(2). Mental Health in Schools Training and Technical Assistance Center. Available: http://smhp.psych.ucla.edu/qf/burnout_qt/spring02.pdf

U.S. Census Bureau. (2009). Current population survey. *Annual social and economic supplements.* Washington, DC: Author.

Vevea, R. (2011, July 14). Report takes aim at CPS' priorities. Chicago News Cooperative. Available: http://www.chicagonewscoop.org/report-takes-aim-at-cps-discipline-policy-budget-priorities

Wilkinson, R., & Pickett, K. (2009). *The spirit level: Why equality makes societies stronger.* New York: Bloomsbury Press.

Woolf, V. (1938). *Three guineas.* New York: Harcourt, Brace & Company.

Yazzie-Mintz, E. (2009). *Charting the path from engagement to achievement: A report on the 2009 High School Survey of School Engagement.* Bloomington, IN: Center for Evaluation & Education Policy, Indiana University. Available: www.indiana.edu/%7Eceep/hssse/images/HSSSE_2010_Report.pdf

Index

Information in figures is indicated by *f*.

About the Authors

Yvette Jackson is internationally recognized for her work in assessing and capitalizing on the learning potential of disenfranchised students and is a leading expert in the cognitive mediation theory of Dr. Reuven Feuerstein. Her research in cognitive development and the impact of neurobiology and culture on intellectual development, learning, and achievement is reflected in her book *The Pedagogy of Confidence: Inspiring High Intellectual Performances in Urban Schools,* published by Teachers College Press.

As director of gifted programs for New York City Public Schools, Dr. Jackson designed the New York City Gifted Programs Framework. She later served as the executive director of instruction and professional development for the New York City Public Schools. She currently serves as chief executive officer of the National Urban Alliance for Effective Education, founded at the College Board and Teachers College, Columbia University. She works with school districts to customize and deliver systemic approaches to reversing underachievement, engaging and accelerating student learning, and eliciting high intellectual performances. She has been a visiting presenter at Harvard, Columbia, and Stanford Universities in the United States; the Feuerstein Institute in Israel; the Conference of ANEIS (Associação Nacional para o Estudo e Intervenção na Sobredotação) in Portugal; and Thinking Schools International in the United Kingdom. She may be reached at yjackson.poc@gmail.com.

Veronica McDermott received her BA and MA in English from SUNY Stony Brook, earned a Professional Diploma in Administration from Long Island University, and completed her doctoral work at New York University. She began her career in the public schools of Long Island, New York, in 1970 and has worked in numerous educational roles ever since, including superintendent of schools, assistant superintendent for curriculum and instruction, principal, district director, dean, and classroom teacher. She has taught, presented, and consulted for school districts, colleges and universities, and national and international organizations, and she has written for many national and local publications.

Dr. McDermott continues to focus her efforts on school transformation, social justice, and equity through her work as regional director with the National Urban Alliance for Effective Education. She is a frequent contributor and faculty member at conferences and workshops dedicated to the role of leaders and leadership teams in school transformation. Her most recent articles were published in *ASCD Express* ("Student Radio: Magnifying Voices, Preparing a Future," 2010) and, with Yvette Jackson, in *Educational Leadership* ("Fearless Leading," 2009). She may be reached at veronica.mcdermott@sympatico.ca.